IRA
WEALTH

PATRICK W. RICE
with JENNIFER DIRKS

SQUAREONE
FINANCE GUIDES

The investment strategies presented in this book are based upon the research and experiences of the author in his many years as an investor and an investment advisor. As you make your own investments, the author and publisher strongly suggest consulting appropriate professionals in the fields of law, real estate, and finance.

Because no investment strategy is foolproof, the authors and publisher are not responsible for any adverse consequences resulting from the use of any of the strategies discussed in the book. However, the publisher believes that this information should be made available to the public.

COVER DESIGNER: Phaedra Mastrocola
IN-HOUSE EDITOR: Joanne Abrams
TYPESETTER: Gary A. Rosenberg

Square One Publishers
115 Herricks Road
Garden City Park, NY 11040
(516) 535-2010 • (877) 900-BOOK
www.squareonepublishers.com

Library of Congress Cataloging-in-Publication Data

Rice, Patrick W. (Patrick Warren), 1945–
  IRA wealth : revolutionary IRA strategies for real estate investment
Patrick W. Rice with Jennifer Dirks.
    p. cm.
  Includes index.
  ISBN 0-7570-0094-0 (pbk.)
1. Real estate investment—United States. 2. Individual retirement
accounts—United States. I. Dirks, Jennifer. II. Title.
HD255.R525   2003
332.63′24′0973—dc21

Printed in the United States of America

10   9   8   7   6   5   4   3   2   1

Contents

PART THREE
High-Return Investments

PART FOUR
Your Retirement

Appendices

I dedicate this book to Claudia.

*They say that behind every great man
is a greater woman.*

*Well, there is one behind even the not so great.
She is proof of that.*

Acknowledgments

Where to start? Captain Miles started me on this IRA adventure, and while at times I thought that I would live to regret it, I didn't, thank you. Susan Milner, without you as a mentor I would never have followed this course. Jennifer Dirks, we would still be talking about doing this book if you had not taken charge and pushed me to completion. Joanne Abrams, the toughest editor known to man, how can I possibly thank you enough for turning my jumble of words into an actual book? Tom Anderson, CEO of PENSCO Trust Company, and Amiram J. Givon, a gifted pension plan attorney of the law firm Sideman & Bancroft, thank you for your technical review and invaluable assistance, and for just being there for the millions of people who need the services of competent, qualified professionals to help them pilot their self-directed pensions. Lori, my right-hand woman, you already know how much help you have been. This is another one of those compliments in lieu of a raise. Rudy Shur, publisher of Square One, thank you for not being afraid to take on a new author with something to say that you knew nothing about until it was actually written. I appreciate the lively discussions we have had on the subject. And to Mrs. Johnson, my eighth grade English teacher, "Yes, it's really me."

Chuck Chatham, I miss you terribly. You did so much for me while you were with us that it is impossible even to define. I know, though, you would be saying, "Good job son." Hold the gates open and say a good word for the rest of us.

Patrick W. Rice

A Note On Gender Usage

When making your IRA investments, your attorney, real estate broker, accountant, and other members of your crew are just as likely to be female as male. However, to avoid long and awkward phrasing within sentences, the publisher has chosen to use male pronouns throughout the book when referring to these professionals. This decision was in no way meant to diminish the skills and contributions of the many fine female professionals now working in the fields of law, real estate, and finance.

Introduction

Bookes give not wisdome where none was before,
but where some is, there reading makes it more.

—SIR JOHN HARINGTON (1561–1612)

T he system that I am about to explain will provide you with
a terrific alternative to the stock market. You can control
your own destiny by using a program—available to anyone
with an Individual Retirement Account (IRA), Education IRA,
Keogh plan, Savings Incentive Match Plan (SIMPLE), or Simplified Employee Pension (SEP)—that will enable you to invest in
real estate and real estate-related products and grow your money
in a truly secure manner. With this system, spelled out in these
pages, you will be in charge.

I am an investment real estate broker. For many years,
through my employment at banks, I helped file account holders'
money into "safe investments." Yet I continued to see bankers
getting richer, and account holders making few gains, if not getting poorer. These account holders had trusted the bank with all
of their retirement funds, and then saw their retirement savings
nosedive with the stock market or creep up only slightly with
mutual fund gains that were obliterated by "transaction fees."
Then one day, almost by accident, I stumbled on a way of investing retirement funds that would allow account holders not only

to secure a return on their investments, but also double, triple, or even quadruple their money. And these gains would be either tax-deferred or tax-free!

I found a way in which people could take control of their finances while backing their investments with the security of real estate. Even then, in 1987, the ability to self-direct retirement funds for IRA wealth through real estate had been around for fifteen years or so. But although I was in the "business," I hadn't known about the phenomenal impact that such investments could have on personal wealth. At first, my employers at the bank were adamant: "You can't do that here," they said. But I soon found out that there weren't any rules to keep me from investing IRA funds in real estate. Rather, it was downplayed by the bank—as it is by many banks and other administrators such as stockbrokerage houses and insurance companies—because the bank made money only by selling its *own* product to IRA account holders.

So instead of working with banks, I started working directly with account holders, and set out to find the best ways to invest IRA funds in real estate. This book will teach you what I've learned. It will tell you how to use your IRA to invest in real estate products. It will show you how to invest in land, rental houses, shopping malls, apartment complexes, and even businesses using this ready source of funds—without penalties and often without taxes on the gains. It will explain how these simple investment strategies can make an amazing difference in your financial well-being.

An estimated 42 million United States households—or 40 percent of the country—now own some type of Individual Retirement Account. But because the concept of investing IRAs in real estate is so misunderstood, less than one percent of IRA account holders take advantage of the wide range of investment products available to them. Instead, they let their money sit in investments that grow at less than 5 percent each year, or more often shrink by 5 percent. And that doesn't even count losses from paying out administration fees.

The Baby Boomers will soon be cashing in their pensions, and it's those rapidly shrinking IRAs that are supposed to sustain them in their golden years. Whether or not you're a Baby Boomer, you are probably asking certain basic questions. Will you be able to maintain your current standard of living during retirement? Is your pension safe in your employer's hands? Will Social Security and Medicare be available and sufficient when you retire? With corporate downsizing, pension fund raiding, stock market crashes, and rising costs, it's easy to be apprehensive about your financial security. Too often, seniors who looked forward to a secure retirement find themselves waiting in the food stamp line instead of the cruise ship line.

It's time to stop this downward spiral and start taking your financial future into your own hands. Ask yourself this: Whom do you want dictating your standard of living during your retirement years? Do you want a suit-and-tie banker, an anonymous stockbroker, or an overworked employer controlling your destiny? Or do *you* want to be in control? Remember that administrators work for a fee; you work for your retirement.

IRA Wealth is all about taking charge of your tax-deferred or -exempt pension and making investments which will insure that you spend your retirement years not counting pennies, but counting memories. This book will show you how to truly diversify your portfolio—and how to secure it at the same time. When people talk about diverse portfolios, all they're usually talking about is stock. What I discovered is the real way to diversify.

This book is divided into four parts. Parts One, Two, and Three each discuss one stage of a progressive investment strategy that moves from start-up, to conservative investment, to investment for rapid growth. Part Four guides you in making any adjustments to your IRA investments that may be necessary directly before or during your retirement. Each section of the book will take you one step closer to accumulating tax-deferred or -exempt dollars in your self-directed pension, at rates that are truly mind-boggling.

Part One of *IRA Wealth* explains the fundamental concepts you need to know, and helps you launch your new self-directed pension plan. First, in Chapter 1, you'll learn the basic rules of investing IRA funds in real estate. Then, in Chapter 2, you'll discover the best investment strategies based upon your retirement needs, your available funds (there may be some you don't even know about), and the time you have before your retirement begins. These initial chapters will help you establish your starting point and destination, and plot the course that will allow you to get from one to the other.

Although I'm a firm believer in taking hold of your retirement future by "self-directing" your investments, there will definitely be times when you need help. The services of an attorney, a financial planner, and other qualified professionals are vital to obtaining IRA wealth. In Chapter 3, you'll find out when professional help is necessary, and you'll learn how to make the best (and most cost-effective) use of the advice you obtain.

Part Two of this book is written for people who want low-risk investments, or who don't want to take all of their money and put it into something they're not sure of. Whether you're a beginner or an experienced yet conservative investor, this section will teach you the easiest and most basic real estate investments.

Most American investors understand the fundamentals of purchasing or selling the family home. What they don't know is that they can buy property with their IRA and enhance their retirement savings at the same time. In Chapter 4, you'll learn how to research, select, purchase, rent, and eventually sell a number of different properties, from a retirement house or condo to a commercial building. You'll even discover the ins and outs of financing a property when your IRA simply doesn't have adequate funds to cover the purchase price. The possibilities are endless, and all of them—if done wisely—can add to your IRA wealth.

Not ready to buy that retirement villa? Fortunately, many other alternatives are available. In Chapter 5, you'll discover how to build your IRA through notes backed by real estate. The purchase and sale of notes can be quite rewarding. And once you've learned a few basics, you'll find that notes can be a safe and secure means of growing your IRA.

Chapter 6 covers nontraditional investments, such as options, tax sale certificates, and judgments. These can be relatively low in risk, yet high yielding—as long as you understand each investment and take the right approach.

Chapter 7, the final chapter in Part Two, will show you how to loan money to a family member-in-need via your IRA. Similarly, you will learn how to rent IRA-bought property to relatives and buy real estate with relatives—all while staying within IRS guidelines.

It's important to understand that whenever money changes homes—when it moves from your pocket to someone else's pocket—there is risk. With each of the investment strategies mentioned above, I describe the risk and explain how to limit it—or, for the more adventurous, how to increase the reward by making a few simple changes in the deal.

Part Three of *IRA Wealth* was written for people who understand that some risk may be required to have a higher return. First, in Chapter 8, you'll learn how to use your IRA to create a regular and often high income stream by buying real estate-backed papers that aren't in first "payback" position, or by buying high-risk property. While high-income streams of all types can be purchased with an IRA, you must know what you are doing if you are to protect your principal and reap the greatest rewards. Chapter 8 will show you how it's done.

Chapter 9 provides the ultimate investment vehicle for the knowledgeable investor who wants to increase retirement funds to the max. This chapter will show you how to tap into one of the most rewarding and popular investments of recent years: the real estate partnership. Anecdotal examples include forming a limited liability company (LLC) to develop a small neighborhood shopping center.

Finally, in Chapter 10, you'll see how to buy yourself a job. Yes, you read that right. Who hasn't heard someone say, "If only there was some way to keep our company from going out of business!" Well, quite often, there is. Using the strategies presented in this chapter, a company's workers can come to the rescue, using the IRAs of key employees to make the purchase. And, yes, workers can use discretionary funds along with their IRAs to make the deal work.

According to the rules that govern traditional IRAs, once you reach a certain age, you must begin making withdrawals from your retirement fund. But how can you do this if your money is tied up in real estate and notes? Part Four guides you in reviewing and adjusting your investments prior to retirement so that you can enjoy the fruits of your labor while fully complying with the law.

At the start of this Introduction, I mentioned that the strategies presented in this book can also be used to invest money held in Keogh, SIMPLE, and SEP plans. This is true. Be aware, though, that for simplicity, I have used the generic term *IRA* when referring to your account. Also be aware that while the rules regarding investments are largely the same for all of these plans, there are variations—especially when dealing with SIMPLE plans and multi-employee SEPs. Therefore, if you have something other than a traditional, Roth, or Education IRA, you'll want to contact one of the administrators listed on page 227. They should be able to explain the regulations that apply to your particular pension plan.

Over the past twenty years, I've discovered systems for growing wealth by leveraging it with the security of real estate. Through speeches at real estate conventions and workshops at bank branches across the country, I've shown thousands of real estate and retirement fund investors how to help their clients invest for the first time. And through my firm, IRA Resource Associates, Inc., I've personally helped thousands of people take the same step. Now, this book will share with you the techniques that I've used to help people just like you build IRA wealth.

Let this book inspire you to create your own retirement wealth. May your retirement years be golden, bountiful, and filled with happiness. See you on the cruise ship.

PART ONE

The Elements of Investing IRA Funds in Real Estate

Congratulations! You have decided to take control of your future—to build IRA wealth and security through self-directed investments. Part One will show you just what it takes to get started. In the following chapters, you will read the real-life adventures of seafarer Captain Miles. You will learn of his retirement goals, of the strategies he used to reach his goals, and of the crew members who helped him along the way. Captain Miles is not a fictional character. He exists, and he made his retirement dreams a reality by using the tactics presented in this book. You can, too.

Chapter 1 first explains how The Captain got started by developing a solid investment plan. It then offers the seven important rules that allowed him to chart his course to a financially secure retirement. It takes work to embark on an adventure as important as retirement planning. You must know where you are going and how you are going to get there. Chapter 1 will start you on your way.

The number of years that remain before your retirement has a great bearing on the strategy you should use to reach your goal. Chapter 2 explores the investment strategy that is best suited for each age range and financial situation. Should you use a

traditional IRA or a Roth IRA? Should you choose low-risk investments, or throw caution to the wind and opt for higher returns?
This chapter not only makes specific recommendations, but also
provides the figures you want and need to guide your choices.

Chapter 2 also shows you exactly *why* you should be making
your investments with tax-deferred or tax-exempt money—IRA
funds, in other words—instead of discretionary funds (savings). If
you aren't already convinced that you can create real wealth,
Chapter 2 will open your eyes to new possibilities and set you on
your course to success. It even discusses other retirement income
sources that may be available to you—sources you may not have
considered in the past. You may find that you have far more
money to use for your retirement than you ever imagined!

Chapter 3 is one you'll want to reread every now and then.
That's because this chapter shows you how to put together and
maintain a good crew to sail your retirement vessel. Without a
responsible and responsive crew, you could drift for years without
a chance of attaining the wealth and stability you need to be comfortable in your retirement years. Think back to all you've heard
and read about the real wealth in America. Do you believe that
Donald Trump or any other real estate magnates made their riches on their own? Of course not! They did it by prudently using
the crew members discussed in Chapter 3: financial planners,
attorneys, accountants, real estate brokers, and title insurance
companies. Forget the no-money-down, get-rich-quick schemes.
The risks of taking out loans for these types of investments far
exceed the possible rewards. Do it the old-fashioned way; work
for your wealth, and seek advice from those in the know. I'll
explain how to keep the costs of these advisors down to a minimum—in some cases, down to nothing at all.

Part One was designed to give you the information you need to
start on your voyage, confident that you can reach your destination.
It has been done before. Creating wealth for retirement is as old as
time. The methods have changed somewhat over the years, as have
the laws, but the basics are the same. The government has provided you with a marvelous tool—the IRA. In the following chapters,
you'll begin to learn how to use it to build IRA wealth.

Investing in Real Estate Products

*One of the greatest pains to human nature
is the pain of a new idea.*

—WALTER BAGEHOT, 1876

For the past twenty-five years or so, "The Captain" had led a nomadic life, traveling from country to country, skippering boats for various oil and fishing companies. Along with his seafaring existence came a laissez-faire attitude about retirement. High living in exotic places like Singapore, Africa's Ivory Coast, and European ports around the North Sea did little to help him save for the future. There were just too many distractions. He did, however, participate in an employer-sponsored retirement plan and was able to roll the funds into an IRA when his stint with that employer ended.

Captain Miles came to me to discuss a problem that he saw looming ahead. He was well into his fifties and felt it was time to start cutting back on his travels. He had set up his base camp in Palm Desert, California; had learned to play golf; and yearned for a life with more play and less work. Throughout his working life, his pattern had been to go to sea for six to nine months of each year, and take the rest of the year off. He wanted to cut the sea time back to two or three months for a couple of years, and then retire altogether.

His concern? He worried he would have more time than he had money. Not only was he going to take more time off, but the new love of his life—golf—was turning out to be quite expensive.

His question to me was, "How can I work less and have more to spend?" It's the same question we all ask as we move closer to our golden years. Fortunately for The Captain, he had a few resources he could draw upon and use as a foundation. He had a small inheritance; his IRA; and, eventually, Social Security. What did I suggest? The plan I drew up for The Captain began my first foray into investing IRA funds in real estate.

THE PLAN

I knew that The Captain needed to generate wealth as quickly as possible. His earning years were coming to an end and, other than Social Security, he would have little to sustain his retirement years. He was cutting back on his workload and would require an immediate monthly income to supplement his semiretirement.

We decided on a two-part plan. He would use his inheritance to acquire income-producing investments that would supplement his part-time seafaring. And he would use his IRA to generate wealth for his actual retirement years.

These types of investments, and the many that followed, could have been accomplished with either The Captain's IRA or his savings (referred to as *discretionary funds*)—in this case, his inheritance. The two funding sources, IRAs and discretionary funds, are totally interchangeable in all of the investment strategies outlined in this book. Each investor must simply weigh the benefits to decide which will work best in his or her particular situation. As I will point out in Chapter 2, there are considerations other than the dollar return on the investment.

Captain Miles, always a good man with figures, devised a budget that reflected all the costs—including green fees and lessons—that he anticipated during his semiretirement. He then subtracted the income he would generate by sailing the high seas for two or three months a year. The remaining amount would have to come from investments made with his inheritance.

At the time I met The Captain, his IRA was invested in a money market fund that earned about 5 percent annually—an interest rate pretty common at that time for bank-administered IRAs. In The Captain's case, we needed an investment that would increase his IRA asset value quickly yet safely. We wanted nothing to do with an investment that would risk the principal.

The concept was simple. The Captain chose to participate in an Individual Retirement Account, an IRA, that was the same as everybody else's IRA in that it was a retirement fund set up by an individual. However, instead of allowing a bank or brokerage firm to invest his IRA funds, he chose to self-direct his investments. Specifically, using The Captain's IRA, we purchased an existing mortgage at a discount. (For more information on discounted paper, see Chapter 5.) The mortgage was supposed to continue for seven more years. But because it paid off early, we received the discounted portion six years early. The discounted portion—about $15,000 plus the interest he received over the nine months—provided a $16,923 profit. This turned a $20,000 IRA investment into $36,923, with all of the money going back into the IRA. Not only did the investment far outdistance the money market fund return he had been getting, but it gave his IRA great diversity. Through further investments, also in real estate, we went on to secure a rosy retirement for the good Captain, with enough money for all the golf lessons and green fees he'd ever want or need.

THE RULES

In my work with The Captain, I had gone where no man (that I knew) had gone before. Yet I had uncovered only the tip of the IRA investment iceberg. Since then, I have repeated the results—with annual returns from 12 to 214 percent—for thousands of people who, like The Captain, wanted a better retirement plan. In each case, the specific investments have been slightly different. However, the key has always been to make investments within the rules that govern the investment of IRA funds in real estate products. These rules are well worth knowing. Stay within them, and you will be able to watch your retirement account wealth double, triple, or even quadruple in value in far fewer years than you would expect.

RULE 1

Set Up a Self-Directed IRA

This is the first step to investing tax-deferred or tax-exempt in real estate. A self-directed account can be established with any one of the two dozen or so administrators out there. (You'll learn more about IRA administrators in Chapter 3.) It is a simple matter of filling out a one-page application and sending in a check for $25 to $50. If you already have a traditional or Roth IRA account set up with a traditional administrator—a bank, stockbroker, or insurance company—you'll need to fill out a transfer form in addition to the application form. The transfer form will move whatever assets you want from your existing IRAs to a single new self-directed account.

The advantage of a self-directed account is that it will allow you to take control of your own destiny and call your own shots. When you set up your account with a self-directed administrator, you will be able to take advantage of all the investments allowed by law—*including* those offered by your bank, stockbroker, or insurance company.

RULE 2

If Possible, Transfer Your 401(k) Funds to the New IRA

One very popular way to fund an IRA with a significant amount of money is to roll over your 401(k) plan. When you are terminated from employment—but *only* when you are terminated—employers with 401(k) programs typically give you four options. You can take your retirement funds in cash, and have 20 percent of the money withheld as taxes; you can leave the funds in the plan, although the time frame may be limited; you can roll the funds into an IRA, an option which is both tax- and penalty-free; or you can roll your existing 401(k) into your new employer's 401(k).

In most cases, a rollover into an IRA is the best option if you want to invest in real estate. To do this, just set up an IRA with the administrator of your choice and sign a "direction letter," instructing the administrator of the 401(k) to roll the funds into the new administrator's account. If you're one of the millions who have just become unemployed, this option will instantly give you thousands of dollars to invest in real estate products.

RULE 3

Learn the Internal Revenue Codes That Govern IRAs

The federal rules that will be most important as you make the investments discussed in this book are spelled out in Title 26, Sections 408A and 4975 of the Internal Revenue Code. These rules—which can be found on pages 229 to 248 of this book—primarily focus on what you *cannot* do rather than on what you *can* do. (Other than this book, there are few resources that will tell you what you can do with your IRA.) However, knowledge of these rules will insure that your investments stay well within the boundaries of the law. In addition, you and your crew—your attorney and your accountant, for instance—may want to review Title 26, Section 408, which is the general section on IRA codes. These and any other codes in which you're interested can easily be accessed on the website of the Office of the Law Revision Counsel. (See page 225 of the Resource List.)

To begin, understand that the government has set up IRA accounts so that they hold retirement funds in trust for you. This is not the same as, "It's my money, and I can do what I want with it." The IRA cannot transact business with you, your spouse, your parents, your kids, or your kids' spouses. The IRA cannot invest in a corporation if 50 percent or more of that corporation is owned by you or your IRA. Moreover, you cannot commingle IRA funds with discretionary funds (cash).

Despite the restrictions imposed by the government, many great investment opportunities remain. In the following chapters, for instance, you'll learn about the strategies that will allow you to invest discretionary funds *with* IRA funds, or even to invest IRA funds with relatives.

RULE 4

Learn All You Can About Real Estate Investments

If you are totally new to the world of real estate—or if you are familiar with only home buying, for instance, but know little about buying commercial real estate or real estate-backed paper—you'll want to get up to speed as soon as possible. Sure, your broker will be responsible for finding the properties, and your accountant will be able to analyze potential investments. But only you can make the final decisions about each investment. To make the best decisions possible as the captain of your retirement ship, you'll want to know all you can about the field in which you're investing.

The information in this book provides a great starting place, but should be used as a springboard to gaining further knowledge. For basic information on the buying and selling of real estate, pay a visit to your local library and bookstore. There, you'll find both general books and books on specific types of investments, such as apartment houses. Also take a look at the periodicals sections. Magazines such as *National Real Estate Investor* provide information on a cross-section of disciplines, including construction, development, finance/investment, and more. Publications like this can introduce you to the market and—just as important—help keep you abreast of trends.

As you probably know, the Internet is a great means of gaining information on almost any subject, including real estate investments and IRA law. By using your favorite search engine, you'll often be able to quickly find articles on the topic of your choice. And, of course, websites are always being updated, making the Internet a particularly good means of keeping informed of real estate trends and tax laws.

Finally, if you're interested in acquiring the skills needed to analyze your real estate investments, consider taking a class. Although many investment groups offer courses, my favorite is the CCIM Institute, which offers both an introductory course in commercial investment real estate analysis and four graduate-level courses. I took several CCIM classes many years ago, and they have paid for themselves over and over again. (For information on the CCIM Institute, see the Resource List on page 225.)

RULE 5

Always Do Your Homework

Whether you perform research on each investment vehicle yourself or you hire a professional to do the work, it must be done thoroughly. Unless you are well versed in real estate analysis, I suggest that you hire an expert. Real estate brokers deal with these investments every day. Their services are normally free to you, since the seller traditionally pays the transaction fee. Also, professionals have access to a greater number of investments than you will ever have, which will give you far more investment options that you'd be able to locate on your own.

RULE 6

Always Be Prepared to Act

You will find that the best opportunities are not available for very long. There is stiff competition for good real estate investments, and if you don't move quickly, somebody else will. So don't wait until you've located a possible investment to find a good accountant or attorney to handle the deal. Instead, have your accountant, your attorney, and the rest of your crew preselected and ready to act on your behalf. (Again, see Chapter 3 for information on the use of professionals.)

Naturally, you should also have your self-directed IRA—transferred from any traditional Individual Retirement Account or rolled over from a 401(k) plan—set up and funded. Moreover, I recommend putting all of the IRA money you'll use for your real estate investments in a money market account so that it will be liquid. True, these accounts, which are offered by most IRA administrators, don't provide a high interest rate. However, they will give you instant access to your money, enabling you to move quickly when an opportunity presents itself.

RULE 7

Every Year, Invest $3,000 (or More) of New Money in Your IRA

Anyone who earns income or receives alimony can invest $3,000 in an IRA annually. (Yes, contrary to what many people think, *taxable* alimony—but not a nontaxable item such as child support—is considered earned income for the purpose of making IRA contributions.) Anyone who is age fifty or over can invest even more—up to $3,500. Furthermore, these limits will rise over the next few years. To insure that you have enough money to fund your real estate investments, make the maximum IRA contribution for your age group each and every year.

These are the rules that you should follow when investing your IRA funds in real estate products. If you're a little overwhelmed by some of these rules—or if you're simply not sure of how they should be applied—relax. All of them will be fully explained and put to use in the chapters that follow. By sticking to these rules, you'll discover ways to grow your retirement dollars—just as I've grown them for thousands of clients—potentially anywhere from 12 percent to 200 percent or more annually. Now, it's time to start earning retirement wealth by funding your own retirement home, buying a failing company, or even loaning money to your brother!

Captaining
Your Own Ship

He who receives an idea from me, receives
instruction himself without lessening mine;
as he who lights his taper at mine
receives light without darkening me.

—THOMAS JEFFERSON, 1800

When Captain Miles first came to me, he knew he didn't have the proper compass course for a successful retirement. As you learned in Chapter 1, though, he is living proof that with strategic planning and a little luck, you can change your course and reach a safe and secure harbor in your retirement.

Since most Americans tend to be like The Captain, waiting until late in life before setting up retirement plans, I will address that course in detail in this chapter. However, as you may already know, the best way to grow funds is to start early. So for those readers astute enough to have picked up this book while still young, I will start the chapter by plotting the course for investors who are still in their twenties or thirties. Regardless of your age and your financial situation, this chapter will guide you to an investment strategy that will help you reach the harbor of your choice.

STARTING OUT IN YOUR DINGHY

If you are just starting out in life—if you are in your twenties or thirties—hooray for you! Anyone who has years of productive employment ahead can successfully plan for a secure retirement through IRA investments in real estate. But when you start taking charge of your finances early in life—ideally, in your twenties— you can more easily insure that you and your family will be able to greet retirement with joy, instead of apprehension and doubt.

I would like you to consider a scenario—the first of many I'll present in this chapter. In doing so, please be aware that when discussing IRAs that are invested in certificates of deposit (CDs) or annuities—the type that most people have—I have chosen to give them a 6-percent return. CD and annuity rates have fluctuated from 2 percent (or less) to 6 percent within the past few years, and there's no way of knowing where the rates will be when you read this book. But a 6-percent return—which is at the optimistic end of the scale—will work in contrasting traditional investment returns with typical real estate investment returns.

Now, our scenario. Let's say that you're twenty-five years old and you're able to fully fund your IRA each year—that is, you contribute $3,000 per year, or $250 per month. In addition, as already explained, we'll assume that you're able to make a 6-percent annual return on your investments. By the time you're fifty-five, you will have accumulated $237,175 while investing only $90,000.

Since you can do this well with only a moderate return on your investments, consider how well you could do if you took control of your investments and realized the kind of returns discussed in Chapter 1. Let's change your strategy. This time, your investment yields a 6-percent return for the first five years, and then starts making 12 percent consistently for the next twenty-five years. Why only 6 percent for the first few years? We're assuming that when just starting out, you will have limited funds to invest, and will be able to get only the return that your stockbroker, banker, or insurance agent can obtain for you. It's a sad fact that the less money you have to invest, the fewer your investment options. But even with the unremarkable gains of the first few years, by year thirty, by making smart real estate investments, you will have accumulated $723,998—while investing the same $90,000 contributed to your IRA in the first scenario. Surprising? I hope so. You just made $486,823 more than you would have made had you stayed in that annuity or CD. You can make the choice right now to have someone else handle your retirement funds—or you can decide to do it yourself.

If you need more convincing, look at Figures 2.1 and 2.2. These figures will show you what you would need to do to acquire $1 million by retirement age. Maybe your dreams of retirement don't require $1 million in funding, but stick with me. The purpose of these figures is not to tell you how you can make $1 million—although that would be nice—but to show you how smart IRA investments can help you reach your personal financial goal, *whatever* it might be.

In both the Figure 2.1 and Figure 2.2 scenarios, you're contributing $3,000 a year to your Roth IRA. (More on Roth IRAs versus traditional IRAs later in this chapter.) But in Figure 2.1, you're making a 6-percent investment, while in Figure 2.2, you're enjoying a return of 12 percent. In neither of these scenarios do the IRA

FIGURE 2.1. REACHING $1 MILLION WITH 6-PERCENT GROWTH	
Amount needed at retirement	$1,000,000
Number of years to retirement	30 years
Amount contributed to Roth IRA annually	$3,000
Amount of discretionary income needed annually	$12,061 (after 25 percent tax)

FIGURE 2.2. REACHING $1 MILLION WITH 12-PERCENT GROWTH	
Amount needed at retirement	$1,000,000
Number of years to retirement	30 years
Amount contributed to Roth IRA annually	$3,000
Amount of discretionary income needed annually	$1,430 (after 25 percent tax)

investments alone allow you to achieve your goal of $1 million. In both cases, additional investments with discretionary income (savings) are needed to make up for the shortfall. But when IRA investments yield only a 6-percent return, as they do in the Figure 2.1 scenario, a whopping $12,061 of discretionary income must be invested each and every year. In contrast, when IRA investments yield 12 percent, only $1,430 of discretionary income must be invested annually, in addition to the IRA funds. These figures clearly show the difference between allowing your money to stagnate in CDs, and becoming an active participant in the investment of your IRA contributions.

When you're young, you should choose mostly low-risk investments for your IRA. You have plenty of time, and retirement funds should not be put at risk any more than necessary. Thus, good investments for you would be the type of low-risk real estate purchases discussed in Chapter 4, as well as low loan-to-value notes, which are explained in detail in Chapter 5. The yields on such investments should easily increase your IRA returns to 12 percent or more annually.

Moreover, be sure to use a Roth IRA as your retirement vehicle as long as you are eligible to do so. Don't even consider a traditional IRA if you have a choice. What's the difference between the two accounts? In a traditional IRA, money may be totally or partially tax-deductible the year it is contributed, but any amounts withdrawn are subject to income tax in the year of their withdrawal. In a Roth IRA, the money contributed to the account is taxed as income the year the contribution is made, but is withdrawn tax-free, provided that you wait for five years and you are $59\frac{1}{2}$ or more years of age. So if you use the traditional IRA, when you retire, you'll be required to pay tax on the contributions as well as the gain whenever you take disbursements. You have no way of knowing what your tax bracket will be when you retire, but if it's 25 percent and you have accumulated $723,998 (see page 21), you'll be handing over $180,199 to Uncle Sam. Bad idea. On the other hand, with a Roth IRA, the gain will be tax-exempt. That means *no taxes on the gain*. No, you won't be able to deduct the $3,000-per-year contributions to a Roth IRA, as you would with a traditional account, but in the long run you'll gain more than $180,000! (For more information on the Roth IRA, see the inset on page 24.)

UNDERWAY IN YOUR CABIN CRUISER

If you are already in your forties or early fifties, you may be wondering how your present low-yielding IRA will be able to support you during your retirement. While you have fewer years to grow your wealth than our hypothetical twenty-five-year-old investor, you probably have a number of things going for you that you didn't have when you were just starting out. To begin with, you are most likely making more money now than you did in your twenties and thirties, so you're in a position to put more money away. You also may have a little nest egg from a previous employer's 401(k) that can be put to use.

For many of my clients in their forties, the drawback is that they made their earlier contributions to a traditional IRA rather than a Roth. Since they'd be taxed on the full amount if they decided to roll it over into a Roth IRA, the cost of converting is sometimes too great. The inset on page 24, which explores the Roth account, will help you decide if the conversion would make sense in your particular circumstances. You may find that, as long as you are able to pay the taxes, it would be wise to roll over at least a *portion* of your traditional IRA into a Roth.

Now that we've looked at the pluses and minuses, let's consider an investment scenario. Let's say that you are starting out with $50,000 in your traditional IRA, possibly a combination of annual contributions and a rollover from a 401(k). Let's also assume that you will make your annual contributions of $3,000 for the next twenty years. What would the difference be between receiving the usual 6-percent return, and receiving a 12-percent return by investing your traditional IRA funds in real estate? With a 6-percent return, you will be retiring on $270,714, of which you will probably lose more than $67,000 or so to taxes if you are in the 25-percent income bracket. Not a pretty sight. With a 12-percent return, however, the amount shoots up to $698,472! Of course, you

The Roth IRA

Throughout this chapter, I encourage you to make your real estate investments through a Roth IRA rather than a traditional IRA. The chief reason for this is briefly explored on page 22. However, the Roth IRA is such a valuable investment tool that it merits further discussion.

The Roth IRA first appeared in 1998 as a result of the Taxpayer Relief Act of 1997. It was named after former Senator William V. Roth, Jr. Like the traditional IRA, the Roth allows you to invest a portion of your income in a private plan earmarked for your retirement. However, the similarities end there.

As discussed earlier in the chapter, when you put money in a traditional IRA, the money is usually tax-deductible for the year in which it is contributed. The money contributed to a Roth IRA is *not* deductible from ordinary income. But—and this is an important "but"—if you meet certain requirements, all earnings will be tax-free

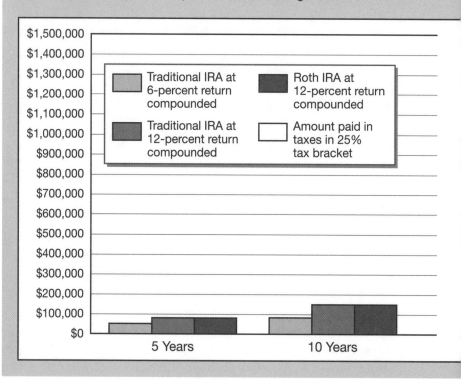

when you withdraw them at a later date, and gains will *never* be taxed! This will make a big difference in your final IRA wealth. How big?

If you look at the graph below, you'll see the growth of three IRAs invested over thirty years. The first is a traditional IRA invested at 6 percent—the type of return that, as discussed earlier, is often made through CDs and annuities. The second is a traditional IRA invested at 12 percent—the type of return that can be made through smart real estate investments. The third is a Roth IRA invested at 12 percent. In each IRA, you make the maximum contribution each and every year. For many years, as might be expected, the two 12-percent accounts keep pace, and both grow at a much greater rate than the 6-percent account. Then, at retirement, comes the tax bite. Both traditional IRAs are sharply decreased, with the 12-percent account losing nearly $400,000! The funds in the Roth IRA, though, are tax-exempt. With no money going to Uncle Sam, every dollar in the Roth account remains available for your use!

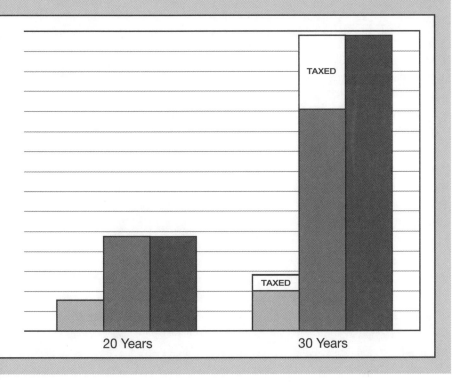

The Roth IRA offers other advantages, as well. If you have your money in a traditional IRA, you must begin making regular withdrawals at age 70½. But minimum distribution rules don't apply to a Roth IRA. This means that if you don't need the money from your IRA at age 70½, your earnings will continue to grow tax-free. In fact, if you so desire and you still have earned income, you can even keep contributing past the age of 70½—a bonus not enjoyed with a traditional IRA.

You are eligible to contribute to a Roth IRA even if you participate in an employer-maintained retirement plan. Like the annual contributions made to a regular IRA, your Roth contributions can be as much as $3,000 if you're under 50 years of age, and as much as $3,500 if you're 50 or older. However, you must meet two requirements. First, you or your spouse must have compensation or taxable alimony income equal to the amount being contributed. Second, your Adjusted Gross Income (AGI) can't exceed certain limits. To make the maximum contribution, the limit is $95,000 for a single individual, and $150,000 for married individuals who file jointly. If your income surpasses these amounts, you can make a partial contribution to your IRA until your AGI reaches $110,000 (if single) or $160,000 (if married). Once your AGI exceeds these upper limits, you may not contribute to a Roth IRA.

The advantages of a Roth IRA are so great that it often makes sense to convert a portion of your traditional account to a Roth—as long as you have several years left to grow your IRA before retirement. This is easily done by setting up a Roth account with a self-directed administrator and converting the funds as desired. Yes, you will have to pay taxes on the amount converted, as Roth IRAs are designed for after-tax dollars. But because the conversion will be counted as income in the year that it occurs, you may not have to make the payment for many months. For instance, if you make the conversion in January of 2004, you will have until April 15, 2005 to make your payment. Moreover, these taxes may, if you wish, be paid with non-IRA assets. Nevertheless, it should go without saying that you should convert only the amount on which you can comfortably pay the taxes. (Your accountant should be able to make the necessary calculations so that you won't face an unpleasant surprise come tax season.) But don't forget that wise real estate investments can enable you to quickly regain the amount you lost—and can keep building your IRA *tax-free!*

will still have your date with the government, which may take as much as $175,000 of your hard-earned retirement income. Still, any way you look at it, a net amount of $523,472 is better than $203,714.

Now, let's make a minor change in your investment strategy and see if it makes sense to you. We're going to assume that because of taxes, you are unable to convert even part of your traditional IRA to a Roth. But that doesn't mean that you can't use a Roth account from now on. So we are going to open up a Roth IRA for you right now, and make all future contributions to the Roth account. We will continue to invest your traditional IRA as before in 12-percent investments, and will invest your new Roth in 6-percent investments for the first five years, and 12-percent investments for the last fifteen years. Your traditional IRA will increase to $482,315. Subtract the $120,579 in taxes, and you have a net amount of $361,736. The Roth, though, will accumulate $204,404—all of which will be tax-free. Add the two investments together, and you will have $566,140. You've picked up another $42,668 just by making your contributions to a Roth IRA.

It's clear, then, that your strategy should begin with the opening of a self-directed Roth IRA. Moreover, your investment strategy should include low-risk investments, such as low loan-to-value notes (see Chapter 5), and relatively low-risk investments, such as options (see Chapter 6). Low-risk investments should be used with your traditional IRA, and relatively low-risk investments should be used with your Roth IRA. Whenever you have the opportunity for a larger gain, put that investment in the Roth. I'll say it again: *The gain from a Roth IRA is tax-free.* You will therefore want to build the Roth account as quickly as your comfort level allows.

THE YACHTING SET

Finally, it's time to address people who are fifty-five years of age or older. In this age group, if you have diligently worked to prepare for retirement by making regular contributions to an IRA throughout your work years, you probably have about $200,000 in your account, and only another ten years or so to make wealth happen.

If you fall into this category, you're going to have to make some drastic changes. Adopting a new strategy, you move into real estate investing and maintain a minimum return of 12-percent for your remaining ten years of employment. During this time, note that you will be able to contribute $3,500 or more to your IRA each year, because the IRS allows an additional contribution for anyone over fifty. (See page 16.) After ten years, the fund will grow to $682,590. Again, take away the 25 percent that you will lose to taxes ($170,648), and you end up with $511,942. This, of course, is far better than the $303,227—$404,302 minus $101,076 for taxes—that would be left if you kept your funds in 6-percent investments. But could you do even better?

This time, let's say that you convert $100,000 of your traditional IRA to a Roth account. Of this amount, $25,000 go to taxes, leaving $75,000 in the new IRA. You then make your contributions to the Roth for ten years and invest both the new Roth IRA and the remaining traditional IRA at 12 percent. Your traditional IRA grows to $310,585 less $77,646 in taxes, for a net amount of $232,939. On the other hand, your $75,000 Roth IRA grows to $294,359 and is *tax-exempt*. With the two accounts totaling $527,298, that's $15,355 more than you made in the scenario that used the traditional IRA only. While this may not seem like a significant gain, in the following chapters, I will show you how to take maximum advantage of the Roth IRA and create even more IRA wealth. What you should remember is that you experienced no net loss by converting a portion of your funds to a Roth IRA.

In the decade before your retirement, be sure to select a mix of low-risk investments, such as low loan-to-value notes (see Chapter 5); and moderate-risk investments, such as second- and third-position notes (see Chapter 8), and real estate purchases made through limited liability companies (see Chapter 9). As in the example of the forty-year-old investor presented earlier in the chapter, you will want to put your higher-risk investments in your Roth account.

A WORD ABOUT RISK

In most of the scenarios in this chapter, I talk about *low-risk* and *moderately low-risk* investments that have annual returns of 12 percent. If you're like most people, at this point you're thinking that any investments which have such high returns must involve greater risk, and that my scenarios are just too good to be true! So before you get any further into the book, it makes sense to address the subject of risk.

My experience has shown that when investing IRA funds in real estate, a minimum-risk return is indeed 12 percent. Such low-risk investments—low-loan-to-value first-position notes, for instance—have about zero chance of going awry. It is highly improbable that you will lose your interest, much less your principal. Moreover, I have found that you can raise the return to 20 percent and still keep the risk relatively low, and can boost it to 25 or even 35 percent if you're willing to take a moderate risk. It's true that moderate-risk investments, such as the purchase of real estate through LLCs, can put your profit as well as a portion of your principal at risk. But ample due diligence—which you'll learn about in the chapters that follow—can make even these investments fairly safe.

On the other hand, in my opinion, the stock market is *high-risk*. Market gains and losses are not controlled by the common man. There are forces at work that are mysterious at best. More often than not, you cannot predict the rise or fall of a particular stock with any degree of certainty. The typical investor looks to someone else to analyze the stock purchase, and bases his or her decisions on that person's best guess. To me—and to all my clients who nearly lost everything in the market—that's scary. Pension losses during 2001 and 2002, all tied to the stock market, are legendary. Diversify in blue chips, yes. Invest your retirement funds in speculative stocks, I don't think so. It's one thing to go to Las Vegas with a pocketful of money that you don't mind losing. It's quite another thing to gamble with your mortgage or your health insurance money. And that's exactly what's at stake when you bet your retirement money on the market.

Oh sure, real estate investing has its detractors. One of the problems most often cited is the nonliquidity of real estate. Translated, that means it takes time to convert real estate back to cash. Well, that's true. What no one mentions is the *need* for liquidity in high-risk investments. When you invest in a rapidly moving investment vehicle such as the stock market, liquidity is extremely important. You must be able to bail out quickly when your stock takes a dive. But when you are in a slower-moving product—real estate, for instance—you have much more time to get out if needed. The real estate market telegraphs its moves well in advance. If you are attuned to the market, you will have ample time to liquidate. When the risk is relatively low, there is no need for immediate liquidity.

Nevertheless, I have received calls from investors who felt that they had weathered the stock market storm of 2001 to 2002 quite well. One reported, "I've done pretty well, I didn't lose anything." My question to him was, "Was that your goal at the beginning? If so, why did you put your money at risk to simply come out even— to not lose anything?" He would have been much smarter to leave his money in his pocket, rather than putting it at extreme risk only to break even. There were others who said, "Pat, as soon as I recover the money I lost in the market collapse, I want to put it in real estate products." Those initial calls came more than a year ago, and those investors still haven't recovered their losses.

How long will *you* wait? Ask yourself this question: Is it smarter to invest what is left of your retirement money so that it earns 12 percent now, or to wait until you recover your losses from a previous investment? With a 12-percent return, you will have a chance to recover all the sooner.

OTHER SOURCES OF RETIREMENT INCOME

You can have more than one boat. In fact, if you are like most Americans, your retirement income will come from many sources—not just from your Individual Retirement Account.

The first source that usually comes to mind is Social Security. If you are close to retirement age, chances are that you will be able to benefit from your many years of contributions. However, while some experts claim that Social Security can be depended on for decades, the fact is that the future is uncertain. We don't really know if younger workers will be able to collect their piece of the Social Security pie. So, depending on your age, it pays to be cautious in your reliance on Social Security payments.

Company retirement plans, created years ago to help businesses lure and keep promising candidates, are another income source for those lucky enough to have them. For all the bad press it has received over the past several years, the 401(k) is still the retirement plan of choice for most workers. It can offer some flexibility regarding investments, depending on the employer's choices, and can also allow the employee to bump up his or her retirement benefits with additional contributions. When offered the opportunity to contribute to a retirement fund, just do it. I don't care if it is your IRA or the company 401(k). Money invested in your retirement is never a bad decision. True, 401(k) plans do limit your investment choices. But there is going to come a time when you leave your company. At that point, you will have the option of rolling your funds into a self-directed IRA, which will allow you to gain full control of your investments.

Few of us think of inheritance as a source of retirement funding. As Americans get more sophisticated, though, more are setting up trusts and other vehicles to pass their hard-earned savings on to their families. I have many clients who use their trusts to invest in real estate for their retirement as well as for the benefit of their children. This is an excellent opportunity for you to train your children in investment strategies. Since they will be the ultimate beneficiaries of the trust anyway, bring them in on the decision-making process and help prepare them to do the same for their children.

That "extra money" you may have at the end of each month should also be put to good use. For years, one of my children's favorite sayings was, "Do you have any extra money Dad?" "Well," I would say, "I don't have any *extra* money, but I do have some *discretionary* money, and I may or may not choose to give it to you." Instead of giving your "extra money" to your kids now, consider using that money to make more money for your retirement. Naturally, when I refer to "extra" or "discretionary" money, I'm talking about any accumulated wealth outside of retirement plans. It could be an inheritance, saved income, or any other money available for investment purposes. Discretionary moneys can be a great source of funding for retirement. Yes, you will pay taxes on the gains that you make. But any gain is a good thing, and the government seldom makes you pay when you don't make money.

Lastly—and I mean *lastly*—there is borrowed money. When we look toward retirement and retirement investing, leverage can be a four-letter word (loan). Four-letter words are not good. Yes, you can borrow at a low rate, invest at a high rate, and make money. But be careful. Leverage can bite.

As you've seen, there are a number of possible sources of investment income—and the strategies discussed in this book may certainly be used with moneys other than those contributed to your IRA. But in this book, my focus is, of course, on the use of the IRA. Why? Because IRA money is tax-deferred or tax-exempt, which is the quintessential benefit of using a pension plan.

Hopefully, by now you're ready to plot your course and head for a successful retirement. But wait! Although you will be in charge of your IRA, you will definitely need some help along the way. Chapter 3 will explain what "crew" you'll need onboard to get safely to your harbor.

Using Professionals Wisely

Wealth is in applications of mind to nature;
and the art of getting rich consists not in industry,
much less in saving, but in a better order,
in timeliness, in being at the right spot.

—RALPH WALDO EMERSON (1803–1882)

There are times when it is foolish to try to proceed on your own. The financial planner, attorney, accountant, real estate broker, title insurance company, and IRA administrator are vital to obtaining IRA wealth. But to maximize the benefits they offer, you must know when to call on them. And, of course, you must know how to pick the best professionals available for the job. Bad advice initially costs the same as good advice, but in the long run, it can capsize your retirement vessels.

I have read many books on real estate investing which insist that you can do it all on your own, without the help of a real estate agent, accountant, or attorney. As a rule, this is nonsense. When operating without the advice of professionals, you are working in the dark. Are there exceptions to this rule? Of course. If you have expertise in one of these areas—if you are a certified public accountant or a real estate agent—you can, of course, take on the task of one of these professionals. For the vast majority of people in the vast majority of cases, though, the guidance of outside experts is a must.

Let's think back to Captain Miles. When he takes his big cargo ship to sea, do you think he goes without an engineer? The Captain is a knowledgeable skipper. He has changed the oil before and put packing in the rudder. But he is not an engineering *expert,* and he's smart enough to know it. Now, Captain Miles doesn't ask the advice of his deck hand when he's plotting a course, and doesn't ask the cook what impact he thinks the weather will have on their progress. But he does defer to these crew members in their areas of expertise. When making your IRA wealth, you, too, will need the guidance of professionals.

YOUR FINANCIAL PLANNER

Understand that here, I am talking about a true financial planner—not a stockbroker who is paid to pick stocks for you. The ideal financial planner is paid a fee based on the overall health of your investments, not on individual trades or acquisitions. This type of planner will be your first mate on the good ship *Retirement.* Like any able first mate, the planner will double-check your decisions and suggest corrections to your course.

You and your planner should meet to discuss the overall health of your investments at least once a year—more often if and when you decide to change course. Whether or not you admit it, you are on a timetable; you have only so many years left until your retirement. Your financial planner will be able to help you determine your course based on your timetable and on the current state of your IRA. You, however, will be the master of your ship. And to you will fall the ultimate responsibility of keeping the ship safe and secure.

Remember that the best planners get paid only a percentage of the assets you hold. If the assets are reduced due to loss, the planner will make less. If the assets increase, the planner will make more. But the planner will not make money every time you make a move. The brokerage community has been fighting the issue of *churning*—trading only to collect a brokerage fee—for years.

While there is nothing inherently wrong with a professional who collects a fee from a client in exchange for each individual service or product, it is natural to question that person's motives.

Perhaps you are already using a financial planner who will be able to counsel you as you build IRA wealth. If not, a good first move would be to ask your other advisors or friends whom they recommend. If your friends can't supply any leads, try contacting an industry association. Groups like the Society of Financial Service Professionals, the Financial Planning Association, and the National Association of Personal Financial Advisors can send you lists of financial planners in your area. (See the Resource List on page 223.)

Once you have the names of a few financial planners, arrange a meeting with each candidate so you can determine who would best meet your needs. Begin each interview by checking the planner's certification. You'll want to find someone with one or more of the following credentials:

❑ **Certified Financial Planner (CFP).** The CFP designation means that the individual has had at least three years of work experience, has completed an approved course of study, and has passed an exam given by the Certified Financial Planner Board of Standards.

❑ **Chartered Financial Consultant (ChFC).** This designation is awarded to those who have successfully completed a course of study and passed exams offered by the American College in Bryn Mawr, Pennsylvania.

❑ **Certified Public Accountant (CPA) certified as Personal Finance Specialist (PFS).** Individuals who have only a CPA designation have passed examinations on tax preparation and accounting. Those CPAs with a PFS designation, however, have also met specific requirements set by the American Institute of CPAs.

Of course, the necessary credentials are only part of the story. During the interview, you'll also want to make sure that the planner has a broad base of investment knowledge. He should either have a basic understanding of all the investment vehicles you choose to use, or be able to easily access the necessary information. You'll also want to make certain that the planner you choose understands the role you want him to play, and is willing to play it. Clearly explain that you intend to be the master of your retirement ship, and that the planner's role is simply to make suggestions for compass settings and course corrections along the way. Above all, take your time and select well. Don't sign on the first candidate you interview—even if he is your brother-in-law.

YOUR ACCOUNTANT

With any luck, you will go beyond the initial buying and selling of simple houses and lots, and delve into the purchase of notes, as well as investments in income-producing properties. I say "with any luck," because this is where the real money is made in real estate. Purchasing a lot and waiting for it to appreciate in value is much like purchasing a blue chip stock. Eventually, it will make money, and it will certainly keep your initial investment safe. But at what cost to your retirement wealth?

The accountant is the ship's engineer. Just as the engineer makes sure that there is enough fuel to make the ship run, the accountant must make absolutely certain that the numbers add up. Do you know how to discount a mortgage to yield a net present value? The accountant does. Do you understand a profit and loss or income statement? The accountant does. Can you look at a pro-forma statement and determine if it falls within acceptable guidelines? The accountant can.

If you are able to comfortably assume the responsibility of analyzing future transactions, by all means do so. But if you are not quite sure of your abilities, find an accountant who's familiar with real estate, and let him know what his role will be in your crew. He is not there to review the transaction for its legality— that's your attorney's job. He is also not there to plan the strategies that will allow you to reach your goals—that's the job of your financial planner. The accountant's job is analysis. Some of the most profitable transactions I've made have been an analyst's nightmare. It requires a tremendous amount of imagination and creativity to structure certain real estate transactions. (I'll describe these later in the book.) So you'll need an imaginative and creative accountant to understand and explain them. These accountants are out there. Your job, of course, is to find them.

Begin your search for an accountant by asking friends for names. If that fails, request recommendations from your banker or local business owners. If you're still stymied, contact a real estate agent who deals with investment properties. In fact, this last resource may be the best of all, as it may most easily allow you to find someone with a knowledge of real estate investments.

Once you have the names of a few accountants, start interviewing. This will give you a chance to determine if a candidate has the background you need. Be wary of accountants who claim to be able to do it all, though. Anyone who is a jack of all trades is likely a master of none. You need a specialist who truly understands real estate, and who understands what you are trying to do through your real estate investments.

Should you demand that your accountant be a CPA—a Certified Public Accountant? This certification shows that the individual has met certain educational and/or experience requirements, and has passed the CPA examination in your state. While the CPA designation does indicate a level of knowledge, I don't view it as being absolutely necessary. A solid understanding of real estate investments is far more important.

At this point, you might be wondering if it would be a good idea to find someone who can act as both your accountant and your financial advisor. After all, if a CPA has a Personal Finance Specialist designation (PFS), he should be able to fill both roles, right? While this may seem to be a good idea—especially if you find a smart professional whom you really like—generally, it is not wise to have one person wear two hats. You want an accountant to counsel you on the individual investments, and a financial planner to provide an objective overall assessment of your investments. If your accountant is also your financial advisor, he may not be able to give you the unbiased feedback you need to keep your ship on course.

YOUR ATTORNEY

In my twenty years in this business, I have truly seen the good, the bad, and the ugly in attorneys. But the fact is that there are times when you cannot proceed without them. I liken the attorney to the ship's cook. The cook is told what to prepare and when to prepare it, and then produces the desired dishes according to existing recipes. Similarly, you choose your investment moves, and it is your attorney's job to prepare the proper documentation according to the law. The attorney must make sure that all documents surrounding the investment—both those already in existence and those that he drafts himself—are sound in the view of the court. In some states, attorneys have other functions, as well: They are responsible for having the title to the property researched and for closing the transactions.

Attorneys specialize in particular types of law much as doctors specialize in specific areas of medicine. Yes, there are those who are general practitioners and try to be all things to all people. However, if you are investing in real estate, you should find a real estate attorney who understands real estate law and its consequences. For some complex transactions, you may also need an attorney who is familiar with those IRA-related rules that can affect real estate investments. If you are now using a good general practice attorney, he will be the first to refer you to a specialist when he gets in over his head.

You should be able to find a good real estate attorney through your bank or real estate broker, or through other real estate investors. If this strategy fails, contact your county or state bar association. (An Internet search or a walk through the Yellow Pages should quickly guide you to the phone number.) Most bar associations have referral services that will help you find a local attorney with the desired area of expertise. Just be aware that the good lawyers with the appropriate experience are very busy. If you reach an attorney who is able to see you the very next day, he may not have the skills you need.

When you find a real estate attorney with whom you can work, be sure to give him explicit directions regarding his role.

Remember that you are the captain of this ship and the attorney is but a recipe reader. In my experience, the good attorney turns into the bad or even the ugly when he does not know where to stop—and that almost always occurs because he wasn't initially given the appropriate guidelines. Instead of doing what he was trained to do, he then steps into the role of financial planner or accountant, and begins reviewing transactions for their worthiness. But don't blame the cook. If you don't tell him what you want, he won't be able to give it to you.

YOUR REAL ESTATE BROKER

Your real estate broker is the deck hand on your crew. I call him the deck hand because many think that of all the crew members, he is the one most easily replaced. But, as Captain Miles could tell you, a good one is truly irreplaceable. He knows his way around the ship like no one else. He looks over the engineer's shoulder and fills in when help is needed. He stands watch on the bridge and navigates with the first mate. He even does time in the galley when the cook is seasick.

A good real estate broker is a good forager. He has the ability to find opportunities that no one else can. Why? Quite simply, he is exposed to many more than you could ever see. Each month, for instance, I attend marketing sessions with other investment real estate brokers. In any one day, I may be exposed to as many as five hundred opportunities. Not all of these, of course, are good opportunities, but the sheer number of them increases the odds of finding an exceptional property. When was the last time you were able to choose from five hundred prospects?

Your real estate broker is also the most cost-effective of all your crew members. The fact is that you may not have to pay him anything because the traditional real estate broker is paid by the party who's *selling* the product. So you can take full advantage of the broker's abilities to bird-dog the type of properties in which you're interested without being on the clock. Not your clock, anyway.

To find an experienced, reputable real estate broker, look for one with the appropriate specialty. If you are interested in adding rental houses to your IRA, look for a broker specializing in houses. If, instead, you want to add apartments to your investments, look for someone who understands that area.

To begin your search for a broker, get referrals from other real estate professionals. If they fail to provide leads, one of two excellent professional associations should be able to help you out. The CCIM Institute, for instance, can help you locate experts in the disciplines of commercial and investment real estate. The CCIM designation—Certified Commercial Investment Member—indicates that the realtor has successfully completed an extensive course of study, and has had actual experience in commercial real estate transactions and consultations. (See the Resource List on page 225 for contact information.)

The National Council of Exchangors (NCE) can also help you find a real estate expert in your area. NCE members who have obtained the EMS (Equity Marketing Specialist) designation have achieved a high level of education in real estate counseling, real estate taxation, real estate financing, and other important areas of the field. These professionals will be able to find the investments you want, and to perform the research you need to safeguard your retirement income. (Again, see page 225.)

Once you've compiled a list of candidates, begin the interview process. Have each interviewee submit a resumé of his past work, and check his references. Never forget that time is money, and that an unskilled broker will cost you money in time. You want someone who can cut to the chase.

YOUR TITLE INSURANCE COMPANY

No real estate transaction would be complete without the title people. It is these critical members of your crew who insure that the title to the property is clear of lien and that the documents are in place, signed properly, recorded in a timely fashion, and distributed to the right parties. All of the work accomplished by your other crew members comes together in the office of the title people.

If you have never worked with a title insurance company, it is worthwhile to take a moment and understand its function. It is this company's responsibility to search the chain of title on a specific property, and make sure that there are no defects that could restrict you from taking the whole title—taking full ownership, in other words. Prior to *closing*—the act of transferring ownership of a property from the seller to the buyer—the title company provides a preliminary title report. This lists the "exceptions" to taking full title, meaning that it lists anything that might have claim to part of the title, such as liens, neighborhood pass-throughs known as "right of ways," etc. Your examination of these reports is a critical part of your research into each investment.

It's worth noting that no real estate transaction, from the purchase of a house to the purchase of a mortgage, should ever be consummated without *title insurance*—a policy that guarantees that when you buy the property, the sale will not be jeopardized by any legal defects in the title. During my twenty-five years in this business, I have had to collect on title insurance only twice, but the payoff made it well worth the cost of years of premiums. Good title company agents are invaluable because of the experience they've gained in completing similar transactions thousands of times. They will recognize an important issue that you overlooked, and point it out to you *before* closing.

Now that you know what a title company does, it's important to understand that title searches are handled differently in different states. In *abstract states*—found mostly on the East Coast and in the Midwest—the buyer's attorney is responsible for having the title search completed. In these states, the attorney prepares an *abstract of title*, which is a historical summary of the property's title that goes back to the first owner. Neither the buyer nor the seller works directly with a title company.

On the other hand, in *title states*—typically found on the West Coast and in the Rocky Mountain region—the buyer of the property works directly with the title company, which researches the property only to the last time title insurance was issued. In these states, by the way, title companies can also act as *escrow agents*, meaning that they can hold earnest money pending fulfillment of contract conditions. They can also conduct closings—a task that must be performed by attorneys in abstract states.

If you live in an abstract state, you needn't worry about finding a title insurance company, as your attorney will take care of that for you. If you live in a title state, you'll be glad to learn that title insurance companies are relatively easy to find, and that most do a good job. Any experienced real estate broker will be able to provide the names of a few reliable title insurance companies. An Internet search for "title insurance" will also give you the names of several companies from which to choose.

YOUR IRA ADMINISTRATOR

Your IRA administrator is a vital part of your retirement plan. Choosing the correct administrator is crucial to accomplishing your goals. One size does not fit all. My clients use many different administrators, depending on what it is they want to accomplish and where they want to accomplish it geographically.

Please note that throughout this book, I have chosen the term "administrator" to designate the company that has responsibility for the operation of your self-directed IRA. However, be aware that I do not recommend the use of the true stand-alone administrator—an unregulated company that uses outside banks or trusts to hold the documents of title. Instead, as your administrator, you want a trustee or custodian that can review the documentation of each investment vehicle; compile the paperwork necessary for each transaction; file the paperwork with the IRS; and hold cash, title to properties, and all other assets of the self-directed IRA. In most cases, modern custodians and trustees have their own administration departments, and therefore serve as both the plan administrator and the trustee/custodian. You can choose either trustee or custodian, as each will provide about the same basic services. Moreover, both types of companies are highly regulated by the Internal Revenue Service, federal or state banking commissioners, and/or other government regulatory agencies. This means that government authorities oversee the firm's operations as a means of protecting the investors' money. Unless you're the type of person who drives without a seat belt, you'll value the safety of dealing with a regulated company.

As discussed earlier in the book, banks, brokerage firms, and other companies that administer most IRAs are not interested in managing self-directed IRAs, simply because they want to sell their own products—stocks and CDs, for instance—rather than real estate. So, to begin, you'll have to find an administrator who is willing to handle self-directed Individual Retirement Accounts. But that's not all that's involved. Indeed, there are a number of questions you should ask when choosing an administrator for your account. And while a bad choice won't be fatal, it may prove to be quite painful, as transferring to another administrator may involve a fee.

First, ask whether the administrator deals with the types of investments in which you're interested. While the law allows all administrators to accept the same products for an IRA, each can choose the specific properties with which it will work. Almost all allow the traditional investments in annuities, certificates of deposit, treasury deposits, and mutual funds. But, of course, you'll want to find an administrator who also allows real estate. Then you'll want to discover the *types* of real estate in which that administrator deals. Some, for instance, allow only land, while some allow both land and improved properties. Ideally, you'll be able to find a company that allows all of the various assets in which you want to invest your IRA funds. If this is not possible, however, you will have to use multiple administrators.

Another question you should pose is whether the administrator is able to hold a real estate title in the state in which you want to invest your IRA. Some administrators—specifically, trustees—have a list of states in which they are licensed to do business. Be sure to get a copy of this list before you start searching for investments.

You'll also want to discover whether the administrator is flexible enough to consider unique transactions. While you won't be able to determine this ahead of time for every possible investment, it's a good idea to discuss this issue at the start, and get a sense of the administrator's willingness to permit unusual investments.

Let's discuss a problem I ran into several years ago. I had been using a particular administrator for several years, mainly buying and selling notes and deeds of trust or mortgages within the IRAs of several clients. I then had the opportunity to purchase a real estate contract for one of the IRAs. A *real estate contract*—which is sometimes called a *land sale contract*—serves the same purpose as a mortgage. There is, however, a difference. When a mortgage is used, the title to the property actually transfers to the buyer at the closing, even though the buyer still owes money. In contrast, when a real estate contract is used, the buyer does not own the property until all of the payments have been made. This type of agreement is quite legal and is, in fact, the contract used in most western states.

When I sent the paperwork purchasing the real estate contract to the IRA administrator for processing, it was rejected because the company was unfamiliar with that type of contract. Only after several in-depth discussions with the administrator's management and legal staff was I able to obtain approval of the transaction. Fortunately, the seller of the contract was willing to wait out the process, and the purchase took place about three weeks later. Since then, I have had to discuss a number of other nonstandard transactions with this administrator, and have found the company to be flexible in all cases. Not all administrators are so open, however.

You will also want to consider the durability of the administrator. Will the administrator be in business as long as your IRA is in existence? Several companies have gone out of business over the years—some for poor business practices, some because of fraud, and some because of takeovers or buy-outs. I feel that those who went out of business because of poor business practices had one particular problem: Instead of simply raising fees to cover their expenses, they tried to make up the shortfall by taking on more and more clients. While you may not be able to foresee impending takeovers or to detect fraud, do be aware of the administrator whose costs are well below those of other administrators. As time goes on, service will be the first thing to suffer. Then the company will either declare bankruptcy or be taken over by another company. While this typically will not jeopardize your IRA or its assets, it will cause delays in business transactions and, typically, increases in fees. And, of course, the new company may not have the flexibility of the old one.

Next, you'll want to consider the skills of the personnel. How capable is the staff that backs up the administrator? This analysis is critical, since the nature of real estate investing requires people with a knowledge of the industry. Does the firm have an in-house attorney? Is it able to answer legal questions quickly? Does it have the necessary expertise to understand IRA law? How often does it deal with your type of investment? What is its turnaround time? And lastly, what will happen when your account representative goes on vacation? I have had clients lose out on lucrative transactions for the simple reason that the administrator wasn't able to move fast enough.

The list found on page 227 provides contact information for several companies that can manage your self-directed IRA. Once you've selected a few candidates, set up interviews and make sure to get concrete answers to all of your questions. Don't be afraid of appearing stupid. You are navigating new waters, and will need answers to all of your questions before you chart your course. Too often, because of the frustration involved in finding an administrator willing to manage a self-directed IRA, an account holder settles for the first company he locates—only to discover that he made a bad choice. Of course, administrators can be changed to obtain the benefits needed, but at a price. Companies typically charge a fee of as much as 1 percent of the transferred amount to allow account holders to move to another administrator. Choose the right administrator at the start, and you will save time, money, and aggravation.

WHAT ARE YOUR COSTS?

You've now learned all about the various crew members you'll need to have onboard. Hopefully, you've begun the process of choosing the best ones for your voyage. But how much will you have to pay for your crew?

The cost of everyone except for the administrator will be fairly minimal. In fact, if the financial planner, accountant, attorney, real estate agent, and title company are used judiciously, less than 1 percent of your overall gain will be spent on them.

To begin at the beginning, it's important to understand that the cost of the financial planner is a moving target. The more you make, the more the planner will make. You should be able to obtain a good planner for 1 percent or less of your asset values per year.

You can keep your accountant costs to a minimum by being very specific in your use. Bring in your accountant only after you've compiled all of the figures. Don't use him to do your research for you. Similarly, avoid calling your attorney to get his opinion on the value or worthiness of a product. Use him only to review and draft legal documents. That's what he was trained to do. If used judiciously, even a fairly pricey attorney won't eat into your profits.

Real estate brokers are by far the best "deal." What will you pay for the services of this professional? Nothing. As discussed earlier, your broker will be paid by the seller of the property.

In different areas of the country, the costs of the title company's services are covered by different people. In title states, discussed earlier in the chapter (see page 41), the buyer and seller generally split the cost of the title search, while the title insurance costs are paid entirely by the seller. In abstract states, however, the buyer pays for both the title search and the title insurance. Therefore, you'll want to check with your broker to learn the practices of the state in which you're purchasing your property. However, realize that even if you do have to assume these costs, they will be minimal. Title insurance, for instance, usually costs less than $10 per $1,000 worth of coverage. Also recognize that in many cases, smart negotiations can result in costs being assumed by the seller rather than you.

Finally, it's time to discuss the cost of an IRA administrator. Administrator charges vary tremendously, depending on the specific service provided and the individual administrators. Usually, the charges for setting up the IRA are minimal: $25 to $50. Once the IRA has been set up, asset-based administrators charge a percentage of the amount of the IRA asset, generally around .5 percent to 1 percent of the first $500,000; while transaction-based administrators charge a fee for each transaction, including the liquidation of assets, asset review, maintenance, and more. In some instances, this can mean a fee every time the administrator collects a note payment. Over the years, most administrators have become hybrids—a combination of asset-based and transaction-based.

What does all of this mean in terms of actual fees? Because of the different ways in which fees may be structured, a $100,000 IRA account may cost as little as $500 or as much as $1,500 yearly. While this may sound like a great deal of money, be aware that if you currently have your IRA at a stockbrokerage house, you are probably paying fees of between 3 and 6 percent. You may not see it under a heading called "fees," but it's there. When you send a $10,000 check to your broker to buy stocks, and he buys shares valued at only $9,400, what do you suppose happened to the other $600? When the costs of trades are recognized, you can see that the .5- to 1.5-percent fees of the self-directed administrator are well within reason.

Once you have your crew onboard, you'll be able to start your journey toward IRA wealth. Of course, even with an able crew, this voyage may seem intimidating. What should be your first destination? If you're a novice investor who has yet to learn the ropes, or if you know the ropes but prefer to make fairly conservative investments, Part Two should be your first port of call. There, you'll learn about a range of low-risk investments that can help you sail toward a secure retirement.

PART TWO

Lower-Risk Investments

You are in charge now. You have chosen to self-direct the investment of your retirement fund, and must take the responsibility of creating and maintaining your retirement assets. Part Two will tell you all you need to know to start growing IRA wealth through low-risk investments.

Chapter 4 explains the basics of buying real estate with your IRA. Whether you're interested in purchasing a retirement home or a commercial property, this chapter will show you not only how to do it, but how to do it *right*. You see, it isn't enough to buy the perfect home to live in when you retire. That home also has to be a good investment. You are trying to *create* wealth—not just hold onto it. Chapter 4 also provides information on paying taxes on your investment, renting your property, and eventually selling your property.

Chapter 5 tells you what you need to know to invest your self-directed IRA in notes. You will learn how to originate a note by making a direct loan, as well as how to purchase an existing note. And you'll discover how to make every investment safe and secure.

Chapter 6 delves into innovative investments that, while not quite as secure as those discussed in Chapters 4 and 5, are still relatively low in risk. The investments discussed include options, which are one of the most inventive ways to fatten your IRA; tax sale certificates, which are a great way to dip your toe into real estate; foreclosure sales, which provide an interesting investment arena; and judgments, which approach the outer limits of low-risk investing.

Chapter 7 is all about involving family members in IRA investments. I consider this low-risk because of the security you'll enjoy when dealing with family. Unfortunately, many investors avoid such transactions because they fear violating IRS codes, which strictly prohibit making IRA investments with certain relatives. That's why this chapter first explains what a prohibited transaction is. The chapter then goes on to explore the many transactions—from renting property to buying property—that you can make with family members, all while staying well within the law. As a bonus, Chapter 7 fills you in on the Coverdell Education Savings Account, better known as the Education IRA. Did you know that you can contribute to an Education IRA *and* your regular IRA in the same year? And you thought you could put only $3,000 in your retirement account!

Before you jump into Chapter 4, realize that while the investments discussed in Part Two are low in risk, they are not *without* risk. That's one of the reasons it's so important to have your "crew" in place. (See Chapter 3.) Whenever you get to a point where you need assistance, reach out to your crew. The few dollars you spend will be well worth it.

If Part One whet your appetite for self-directed IRA investments, Part Two will begin satisfying it with explorations of safe investments that you can make with the funds in your Individual Retirement Account. Turn the page, and start growing your IRA wealth.

4

Buying Real Estate

*They do me wrong who say I come no more
for every day I stand outside your door. Opportunity.*

—WALTER MALONE, 1903

Can you buy real estate with your IRA? Sure you can! It's true that you can't buy a home to live in right now, but you can purchase a wonderful house for your retirement. Moreover, while you're waiting to retire, you can rent your house to someone else and use the monthly checks to build your IRA. You can even rent it to your brother or your spouse's brother, and help out a family member while enjoying a steady stream of income. (For information on IRA investments that involve family members, see Chapter 7.)

This chapter looks at a range of real estate purchases you can make with your Individual Retirement Account, from houses to condos to commercial buildings to vacant lots. Moreover, it tells you how to acquire that great investment property even if your IRA doesn't have adequate funds for the purchase. Of course, in order to protect your investment and grow your IRA, you have to know what you're doing at each step of the way. This chapter will guide you through the process, from finding the property you want to researching it, buying it, and ultimately selling it for a profit.

WHY BUY REAL ESTATE?

There are many reasons to buy real estate with your IRA. Since you were wise enough to pick up this book, you probably already know one of them—security. There is much more security in real estate than there is in the stock market. Unlike a stock, a piece of land can never totally lose its value. It won't simply cease to exist like so many dot-com companies did a few years back! Sure, values rise and fall in real estate, but they do so at a snail's pace when compared with the rapid ups and downs of stocks, giving you ample time to sell your property if the need arises. Moreover, by fully researching each investment before you jump into it, you will be able to buy your property as values are going up, and sell it when they're near the top.

Naturally, real estate also has a practical use. While a promissory note may provide you with a nice income, neither you nor anyone else can live in it. However, if you use your IRA to buy the retirement home of your dreams, your house will be waiting for you when retirement rolls around. And in the meantime, it can be a great rental for someone else—perhaps even a member of your own family.

This brings to mind another reason to buy real estate: Income. A range of properties, from rental houses to apartment buildings to parking lots, can provide a constant stream of income that will build IRA wealth. Many people think that they don't have the money to purchase income-producing property simply because they don't have adequate discretionary funds (savings). However, often they do have an amazing account—an IRA—at their disposal, ready to finance a slew of profitable purchases.

But perhaps the best reason of all to buy real estate with your IRA is that it can appreciate in value. This is the goal that you should keep in mind as you choose your investments. Unfortunately, many novice investors don't. Consider, for instance, the fact that young people love to invest in duplexes simply because they often live in duplexes. While the duplex may be a nice place to live, it is not a great investment. Why? New duplexes are generally rented by young couples, while older duplexes are sought by perennial renters. This does not result in the rapidly rising rents that create appreciation. Plus, any net income from a duplex usually must be put right back into it to cover repairs and maintenance.

In contrast, consider a parking lot. Sure, it doesn't have the romance of a duplex. But a parking lot requires very little maintenance, and as cities grow, parking prices can skyrocket. Investors who look at the return, and not at the romance, will see their property appreciate and their IRA grow in leaps and bounds.

YOUR CREW

Now that you know the benefits of buying real estate, you're ready to gather your crew. Before you read the discussion below, though, a caveat is in order. It's important to realize that in some states, a specific step in the purchase of property might be accomplished by one member of the crew, while in other states, another professional might take care of that task. The following information on crew members tries to provide the scenario common in most areas of the country. But you must rely on your crew members to steer you through the purchase process as it's practiced in your state.

Wherever you live, the first crew member you'll want to bring onboard is your real estate broker, because he's the one who will be charged with finding the property. If you're interested in buying a condominium or single-family home, any real estate broker should be able to assist you. But if you're looking for a multi-unit building or another type of commercial real estate, you'd be smart to use a real estate agent who regularly handles investment properties. As you'll learn by reading the inset on page 54, you won't want to limit your broker to a single location—unless you're looking for a retirement home, of course. Just tell him to get that great buy anywhere he can find it. Later, of course, your broker will also deliver your offer to the seller of the property. In some cases—when the transaction is a simple one—he will also prepare the contract of sale. In fact, a good broker will guide you through the entire process of purchasing property.

Location!
Location!
Location!

Anyone who knows anything about real estate will tell you that location is a critical factor. In addition to considering what the investment is, you must consider where it is. For instance, while a parking lot is usually a good investment, it becomes a great investment when it's located in an area that's experiencing rapid growth. In such an area, overcrowding can cause parking prices to soar. Now consider an empty lot located in an area with no access versus one located near the exit ramp of a busy highway. Which property would be the best investment for someone interested in building a shopping center? Location makes the second lot a much smarter choice.

Be aware, though, that too many investors think of location in the wrong way. I don't know how many times clients have told me that they want to find investment property within a hour's driving distance of their home or business! While it makes sense to buy a home that's close to your office, it doesn't make sense to choose an investment that way. Instead, select your investment property as you would a stock. When you ask your real estate broker to forage for an investment, tell him what kind of return you're looking for— not where you want the property to be located. Do you need a steady income stream, or are you looking for growth and appreciation? Once you've provided these parameters, allow your broker to find the right investment for you—wherever it may be. Don't limit his search by telling him that it must be in such and such a town or city. Of course, it's true that if the property is located nearby, you'll be able to keep an eye on it. But if the property is located far away, you need only factor in the necessary management expenses and examine the bottom line. Very often, the overall return of a superb investment makes it well worth that added fee.

Will you need your accountant for each investment? As you may remember from Chapter 3, the key to keeping expenses low and profits high is to use your crew judiciously. Naturally, if you run every potential transaction past your accountant, your costs are going to skyrocket. So when handling simpler transactions, I recommend doing the math yourself. For instance, if a rental house provides an annual income of $10,000, and the expenses come to $6,000, you only have to subtract the expenses from the income to find your net income of $4,000. However, you may want to use your accountant to review the documentation on which you based these numbers—income and expense reports, in other words—to insure that they make sense. And in the case of more complicated commercial investments in which you're comparing several properties, you will definitely want to have your accountant review all of the due diligence—the tax returns, income and expense statements, property tax statements, leases, and inspection report. He will then be able to tell you which of the properties show the best returns and will maintain the greatest value over the long run.

Will you need your attorney? Absolutely! Your attorney will be responsible for drafting a number of documents, including the contract, when the transaction is a complicated one; any necessary deeds, such as a tenants-in-common deed; and, if necessary, a promissory note. (To learn more about tenancy-in-common ownership, see page 71. To learn about notes, see Chapter 5.) On most occasions, you will not need your attorney to draft the offer; you can feel safe using your broker to draw that up. In fact, most states have such complicated restrictions and clauses that the draft is a prepared form, and the broker merely fills in the blanks. In the case of a complicated transaction that involves several leases, properties, and tenants, though, you may want the assistance of an attorney. In certain states, the attorney also handles the final closing.

Once the offer is accepted, in most cases, the broker will give all the necessary paperwork to the title company. This company is responsible for performing the title search and, of course, for providing the title insurance. (See page 40, Chapter 3, for further details.)

If and when you rent your IRA-purchased property for income, you may have to add another crew member—a property management company. Why? Some administrators will not allow you to manage the property owned by your IRA. However, as you'll learn on page 76, even when this is the case, a number of options are available to you.

Ultimately, the paperwork will be sent to your IRA administrator, who will (hopefully) approve of and fund the deal—typically, through a wire transfer made directly from your account to the title company. The administrator will also be responsible for filing the appropriate paperwork with the IRS.

TYPES OF PROPERTY

The types of real estate that you can invest in with your IRA are endless! You can purchase nearly anything—as long as you don't use the property as a personal residence or as your place of business. You can also rent the purchased property to anyone who is not a disqualified person, and use the monthly payments to grow your IRA. (To learn about disqualified persons, see Chapter 7.)

Of course, a few types of property continuously top the list of IRA investments. Let's look at each one and explore its pros and cons.

Residential Property

When you think of residential property, the one-family house might be the first type of real estate that comes to mind. But residential property can take several forms, including the multi-family house, the condominium, and the mobile home.

Houses

Because every residence from a one-family home to a four-plex is financed in the same way, most real estate investors place them all in the "house" category. The primary purpose of purchasing one- to four-family housing is to either generate income from rent or take advantage of the property's appreciation over the span of ownership. Another strategy would be to buy a *handyman's special*—a house that requires extensive remodeling and repair—for a low price, and resell it for a profit.

A house that's purchased as an investment must be viewed from a certain perspective. When choosing this property, you won't want to wear the same hat you wore when you selected your own home. The inset on page 58 looks at some of the factors you'll need to consider.

When buying a house with your IRA, you must keep certain rules in mind. You cannot live in the house until you retire. You cannot use it as collateral for any loan—not even a loan on the property you're buying with your IRA. (To learn more about prohibited transactions, see Chapter 7.) But your IRA-purchased house can have many benefits. First and foremost, when rented, the house can provide your IRA with a steady stream of income. Moreoever, when well cared for, houses tend to hold their value, so you will rarely if ever experience a loss. And in many cases, you can buy a house with relatively little money down.

Of course, houses have some drawbacks as well. While they hold their value, they don't appreciate as readily as some commercial real estate properties do. And, of course, there is the hassle of maintaining the property and finding renters. Nevertheless, as the following scenario shows, the house can be a superb investment vehicle.

Buying a House—A Scenario

Let's say that you have decided to buy a rental property—a house. You call your broker and explain exactly what you're looking for, including the age of the property, the price range, and the expected income. Within a few days, the broker locates a good prospect in Galveston, Texas.

The Galveston house is in good condition, and is located in an area where the annual appreciation rate is in the area of 4 percent. The asking price is $100,000. The broker sends you the results of his diligent research into area rents, taxes, and other financial factors, and you see that expenses—including taxes, insurance, and

Should You Buy This House With Your IRA?

Perhaps you already own a home, and feel confident that you know how to select an investment house for your IRA. But your home and your investment property are two very different animals. What factors should be considered when choosing a house for purchase with your retirement account? Following are the key elements that must be kept in mind.

Security

Most of all, you want this investment to be secure. In other words, you want to know that this house will at least hold its value during the time of ownership. What you don't want is a house that is already in poor condition, and that will continue to be neglected during your ownership. This situation will cause you to lose your principal, and that's something you never want to do when making IRA investments.

Cash Flow

You will also want to make sure that this investment will result in positive cash flow. When we talk of cash flow, we're referring to the net income that will be available to your IRA from the rental of your property after you make all necessary expenditures. Naturally, to determine your cash flow, you'll have to look at a number of factors.

First, you must determine the market rent for the house. The market rent is the rent that a comparable unit would command if offered on the market. This is different from contract rent, which is merely the rent stated in the contract. You'll also want to see if the market is going up or down, as this will affect the rent you'll be able to collect in years to come.

Now that you have determined the money that will be coming in, you must assess the money that will be going out. First, make sure that the property is thoroughly inspected so that you are aware of all problems that may cost you money in the short- or long-term. Remember that the IRA is a separate entity from you, and must be able to provide the money for any repairs needed on the property that it purchases. Just as you cannot dig into your retirement account's pockets to make repairs on your own home, your retirement account cannot dig into your pockets to make repairs on its properties.

Now you'll need to correctly compute your tax bill. Remember that your tax bill is based on the value of your home, and may be very different from that of the seller. Many tax authorities refer to the sales price to adjust the market value. If the previous owner bought the house for $80,000, but you are buying it for $150,000, your tax bill may be almost double the previous one. You'll also want to find out if the government is planning improvements to roads, sewers, and parks. These upgrades could result in a new assessment and higher taxes.

Next, you'll want to consider your utility bills. While the previous owner's utility bills will provide ballpark figures, keep in mind that people who pay their own utilities tend to use less water, electricity, etc. than those whose services are included in the rent. Will you be paying your utilities, or will your tenant? This can make a difference.

Finally, consider the cost of the insurance. If the value of the house has gone up over time, your insurance will cost more than that of the previous owner's. When talking to your insurance agent, ask what will happen when the property is vacant between tenants. The cost can go through the roof, because no company wants to insure a vacant building.

It goes without saying that if this purchase would keep pulling money out of your IRA, instead of adding to your IRA wealth, it would not make economic sense. More money must come in than go out. Also keep in mind that if your IRA has inadequate funds to cover expenses, you can put new cash in your account to make up for the shortfall. But if this addition increases your contribution beyond your maximum annual limit, the IRS will slap you with a 6-percent penalty that will remain in effect until the excess cash is removed from the account.

Appreciation

You'll also want to insure that the property you buy will appreciate— increase in value. When considering this, be aware that if your house increased in value last year, that may only reflect inflation, which averages about 3 percent annually. Inflation is not a true indicator of value because it simply shows how much the dollar has weakened.

What, then, are we talking about? Specifically, we are referring to the increase in value due to viable economic reasons. These reasons can include an increase in rent, a decrease in taxes, an increased demand for housing in that area, modernization, the elimination of negative factors within or outside the property, and more. If, for instance, all of your neighbors improved the area by prettying up their yards, that could add 5 percent to the property's value. This is real appreciation, and in many cases, you will be in control of some of the factors that create it. For instance, if you know that you will be able to make cosmetic improvements to the house, you can be fairly sure that your property will appreciate in value.

Depreciation

Depreciation is simply a decline in a property's value. Clearly, you do not want your IRA-purchased property to depreciate in value. When you buy a house with discretionary funds, depreciation can result in tax benefits. But, as you know, your IRA money is already tax-deferred or tax-exempt. Therefore, depreciation has no upside, and will simply result in a loss of some of your initial investment money.

When considering the purchase of a home with your IRA, you'll want to be certain that your retirement account has sufficient funds to prevent the property from deteriorating. Also make sure that the values in the neighborhood are not falling due to social changes or other reasons.

I hope I haven't deterred you from using your IRA to invest in a house. Property is a great means of building IRA wealth! But not all properties are equal. While you don't have to personally like the house you buy with your retirement fund, you want to make sure that the property will not only retain its value, but will increase in value, all the while maintaining a flow of cash that causes your IRA to grow and flourish.

utilities—will total $275 a month. The rent is likely to remain at $1,100 per month. You do your own math. The annual income totals $13,200 ($1,100 × 12 months), and when you subtract the annual expenses of $3,300 ($275 × 12 months), you end up with a net operating income of $9,900. Then you divide the net income by the purchase price, and get a 9.9-percent annual cash-on-cash return. ($9,900 ÷ $100,0000 = .099) (To learn about cash-on-cash returns, see the inset on page 180 of Chapter 9.) This is roughly the return you were looking for—and you know that you have not yet calculated in the expected appreciation.

You ask your accountant to review the figures, and he feels that this is a great investment because with the annual appreciation, your return will be in the double digits. You decide to offer the asking price of $100,000, as it will give you the return you're looking for. While you might be able to pay a lower price, you're not a great believer in offering a lower amount and negotiating upward. Your strategy is to offer what you can afford to pay based on the property's expected returns. If the seller wants to negotiate upwards, you'll ask him to point out the benefits that you overlooked in your projections. You don't worry as much about leaving a few dollars on the table as you do about buying something that gives you the bottom line you need.

The offer is accepted, and the broker prepares the contract of sale. Since the property is in another state, and because the rules of your IRA administrator don't allow the owner of the IRA to manage his own property, you find a management firm and budget the fee into your bottom line. The management fee is 6 percent of the gross income, which brings your net income down to $9,108 per year, or 9.1 percent, not including appreciation. Your IRA will now enjoy a constant stream of income, and someday, when the house is sold, will benefit from a large payoff.

Condominiums

If you feel that you want to buy a residential property with your IRA, but the task of maintaining a house and finding tenants seems too time-consuming, consider a *condominium*—an individual residential unit in a multi-unit structure, where the individual units are owned privately, and commonly used areas are owned jointly. A condominium is often a good investment choice simply because in many cases, it can be placed in a rental pool, meaning that it and all the other condo units are managed by a single individual or company. The manager rents the condos and puts the resulting income in a common fund, which is divided among the separate owners. This takes much of the work off your hands. In addition, the manager is responsible for maintaining both the buildings and the grounds. Keep in mind, though, that the money for this maintenance is collected from the owners. Your IRA has to contain sufficient funds to cover these fees.

Buying a Condo—A Scenario

Let's say you decide to buy a condo in Florida because you eventually intend to use it as your retirement home. Of course, you want a property that will suit you as a home, but you also want it to be a viable investment. For many years before your retirement, you'll be renting the property out, and it must make economic sense.

You call your broker, and tell him the desired area and price range. You also express your preference for a condominium on a golf course. He checks a variety of sources, including websites that list retirement condominiums on golf courses. Soon, he finds two possibilities, and is able to provide you with hard data on each. To make the task of comparison easier, you draw up the table presented on page 63.

You crunch the numbers and find that the returns are similar. But your research isn't over yet. You also read through each property's Condominium Declaration to determine if there are any restrictions on the title. For instance, some state that no more than 50 percent of the project can be rented. You don't want to find this out *after* making the purchase. You also check the condominium association's books to see if they have enough reserves to take care of anticipated common area costs. A lot can happen between now and your retirement, and you want it to be for the better.

With all of your research complete, you choose the second condo. Why? Because it sits on an eighteen-hole golf course, of

	CONDO #1	CONDO #2
Price	$250,000	$275,000
Location	On a 9-hole golf course	On an 18-hole golf course
Rent (income)	$28,000 per year	$31,200 per year
Utility Costs	$1,800 per year	$2,700 per year
Property Tax	$3,750 per year	$4,125 per year
Insurance	$1,500 per year	$1,650 per year
Management Fee	$1,020 per year	$1,554 per year
Condo Association Fee	$2,400 per year	$2,400 per year
Total Net Income	$18,330	$18,771
Annual Return	7.3%	6.8%

course! Yes, as discussed earlier in the chapter, it's important to analyze the numbers and select an investment that will grow your IRA. When returns are this close, though, you can afford to express a personal preference.

How does the purchase benefit your IRA? It receives $18,771 per year until you retire. At that point, if you have a traditional IRA, you'll need to take the condo as a disbursement and pay your taxes. (You'll learn more about that in Chapter 11.) How about that? You now have a retirement home that will build IRA wealth until you're ready to move in and enjoy the links!

Mobile Homes

Most investors overlook the opportunity offered by a *mobile home*—a residential unit manufactured in a factory and designed for transport to a permanent site. (Note that this is different from a recreational vehicle, or RV.) Mobile homes, more correctly known as *manufactured homes,* have been very popular in many areas of the country over the past few decades. These houses offer all of the amenities of a traditionally built home, but sell for a lot less money. Manufactured homes may be transported to a mobile home park, where each individual plot is leased, or to a mobile home subdivision, where the homeowner actually buys the plot on which his house is situated.

When the mobile home first appeared, too many people thought it was a great idea. Overbuilding, along with too-easy bank approval of credit for these homes, caused the market to fail at the end of the twentieth century. Since the mobile home crash coincided with a downturn in the economy as a whole, banks had to foreclose on large numbers of manufactured homes. Not wanting these depreciating assets on their books, the banks—not eager to finance yet another sale of these homes—began offering them for 50 percent or less of their market value as long as the buyer paid cash.

What does this mean to you, the IRA investor? By using the funds readily available in your IRA, you can purchase a mobile home for a fraction of its original value of $50,000 to $70,000. Yet the home's worth as a rental has not been devalued, making it an excellent IRA investment. True, it is a depreciating asset. It will not increase in value. But it will depreciate much more slowly than the old mobile homes did, and in the meantime, your retirement account will receive a constant stream of income.

Buying a Mobile Home—A Scenario

Let's say that you decide to buy a mobile home. You know that you can go to a local mobile home dealership or distributor and ask if they have any foreclosures in their portfolio. They would be happy to assist, as this is how they make their money. Instead, though, you go to your local credit union to see what they have available.

The credit union has several repossessed homes from which you can choose. Since all of the homes are in your area, you take a drive and view them in person. While a couple are in good condition, one is in an especially nice mobile home park, making it a better investment. You ask your credit union for the numbers, and they tell you that although the mobile home originally sold for $60,000, to get it off their books, they are willing to sell it for $30,000. The rent, however, has not decreased. Before the home was repossessed, it was renting for $750 a month, or $9,000 a year.

Similar homes are still renting for that amount. Expenses will include $2,400 for the rental of the lot, property taxes of $700 a year, and insurance of $300 per year. The utilities will be paid by the tenant, and because the home is close to your brother, he will be able to manage the property. Your total net income will be $5,600 per year, giving you an annual return of 18.67 percent.

You decide to buy the home. You know that unlike a traditional home, the mobile home will not appreciate in value. However, your IRA will be able to cover the costs with ease, and the 18-percent return will make your retirement account grow nicely for many years to come.

Commercial Property

A *commercial property* is real estate intended for use by retail, wholesale, office, hotel, or service businesses. The only residences included in this category are designed for more than four families. Apartment houses, for instance, are considered commercial, not residential. Other properties deemed commercial include hotels and motels, resorts, restaurants, service stations, convenience stores, shopping centers, and office buildings.

In some ways, commercial properties are better investments than houses because businesses can afford to pay rents of higher per-square-foot value. Moreover, most commercial lease agreements stipulate that the tenant is responsible for the upkeep of the leased space. This means less work for you. The downside, of course, is increased risk. As a commercial property owner, your income is dependent on the success of your tenant's business. When a house renter loses his job, he still needs a place to live and will try to continue paying his rent. When a business fails, however, the business owner no longer needs a space to rent.

Buying Commercial Property—A Scenario

Let's say that you have decided to add commercial property to your IRA investments, and you give your broker a call. You tell him that you have $400,000 in your retirement account to invest, and that you want a property that provides both security and consistent cash flow. You don't want to take on debt, so your existing funds must be the extent of the investment.

After doing a good deal of research, your broker finds three possible investments. He describes each for you.

The first property is a small apartment building. It consists of seven two-bedroom units in a very nice section of Atlanta, Georgia. The list price is $275,000, and the broker has found that rents in that area are rising quickly. None of the tenants, however, are under lease; all are renting from month to month. After expenses, the building currently has a cash flow of $25,000 per year.

The second property is a small commercial building in Antioch, Maine. It's listed at $325,000, and has had the same tenants for more than ten years. This building is a picturesque 1920s block structure with typical small-town, home-grown tenants, including an antiques dealer, beauty shop, dry cleaner, and drugstore. After expenses, the property has a cash flow of $30,000 per year.

The last property is a Pizza Hut in Malta, Montana. The tenant is three years into his ten-year lease, and has two five-year options to extend. The seller wants $350,000 for the property, and the cash flow, after expenses, is $30,000 per year.

All three properties seem like possibilities, so the broker does *due diligence* for each, meaning that he performs a careful study of the physical, financial, legal, and social characteristics of the property. As part of his financial research, he gathers tax returns, income and expense statements, property tax statements, and leases. At your request, he turns all of his data over to your accountant, so that he can do his magic.

After careful analysis, the accountant replies. The apartment building is showing a return of 9 percent annually. That means that, excluding appreciation and depreciation, there will be an annual return of 9 percent on the invested amount. This is about where you wanted it to be. The inspection report shows the property to be in good condition for its age. However, the accountant notes that because the tenants are not under lease, they can move out at will.

The commercial property in Maine also shows a good annual return—9.23 percent. Moreover, the leases have two years to run. However, the inspection report has determined that work needs to be done on the roof. The accountant also points out that current taxes are being based on the last reported sale, which valued the property at $120,000. If you buy the property for the asking price of $325,000, taxes can be expected to triple.

According to the accountant, the Pizza Hut property has the least profitable return—about 8.5 percent annually. But it has advantages as well, the greatest of which is a *triple-net lease*. This means that the tenant pays all of the property's operating costs, including utilities, taxes, and insurance. The owner of the property receives a net rent. Moreover, according to the lease, the rent increases every two years.

Armed with this analysis, you rethink your options. First, you consider the apartment building. The prospect of rising rents in a growing area is very attractive, and the cash flow is good. However, you are concerned about the possible turnover of tenants, which, you know, can ruin your bottom line very quickly.

The property in Maine has the best cash flow. The shortness of the lease is a concern, however, as is the need to fix a sagging roof at great expense to your IRA. Plus, there is the real possibility of skyrocketing taxes.

Finally, you take another look at the Pizza Hut. The annual return is the lowest of the three, but is still quite respectable. More important are the advantages, which are considerable. First, it has a long-term lease with a national tenant. Second, the tenant pays for *all expenses*. This means that when taxes or utilities increase, your cash flow will not be affected. And, of course, the rent will automatically be increased every two years. Does it bother you that Malta, Montana is far away? Not at all. It's not as if you plan to go there for lunch. Your primary goals are security and consistency in cash flow, so Pizza Hut is the winner.

You call your broker and tell him to make an offer on the building. Since he's working with your IRA's ready supply of cash, he can offer a slightly lower price because the deal is not subject to financing and can close quickly. The offer of $325,000—$25,000 less than the asking price—is accepted. Soon, with the help of a management company, your IRA is receiving $2,300 a month.

Vacant Lots

People buy vacant lots for a variety of reasons. For instance, to protect your own privacy, you may want to buy a lot that's adjacent to your home simply to prevent another house from being built next door. While this would be a smart use of discretionary funds, when buying property with your IRA, you naturally want to focus on purchases that will put money back into your retirement account. Does that mean that a vacant lot can't be a good IRA investment? On the contrary, a vacant lot can be a *great* investment!

Consider first a vacant lot that is in the *path of progress*, meaning that development and industry are moving in that direction, and the property lies in their path. While such a lot may be available for very little, once industry begins to build, the price may skyrocket. Or consider a new subdivision, where the developer is willing to sell the first few lots at a reduced price to pay his bills and finance the development. The value of these lots will eventually go up, making a nice profit for your retirement account. Yet another possibility is an unimproved lot that is scheduled to be rezoned or have utilities brought in within the next year.

While profits realized through vacant lot purchases can be dramatic, it's vital to do a thorough job of investigating any land you buy. Remember that as long as you hold the land, you will have to pay taxes even though the property produces no income. And not all land goes up in value; some of it sits there for many years, stagnating. Before you buy a vacant lot with your IRA, there should be good reason to believe that the land will soon be in demand.

Buying a Vacant Lot—A Scenario

Let's say that your broker calls to tell you about a wonderful prospect. A couple of years ago, a developer he knows purchased 500 lots in a subdivision. The subdivision has a long history dating back twenty years. It started out with 1,300 lots on a lake and golf course. The original developer then fell on bad times, and the land was picked up by another developer. Then there was a foreclosure, and so on. The current developer bought the remaining lots at a low price, and now, builders are buying them for $20,000 a piece and constructing spec and custom homes. The developer wants to step up the sales by adding some amenities and doing some advertising. To accomplish this, though, he needs $390,000. He is willing to sell the lots at $5,000 less apiece than the builders' price in order to raise the needed funds. Research shows that other similar subdivisions in the area have a minimum sales price of $40,000. Once this subdivision gets up and running, the value of these lots should jump to the area average.

You review the information, and have your accountant crunch the numbers. Any way you look at the figures, they look great, so you decide to buy twenty-six lots through your IRA for $15,000 each, or a total of $390,000. You hold the lots for three years, during which your only costs are taxes, which are $150 per year per lot, or $3,900 total. Then the developer agrees to buy them back from you at $35,000 per lot. You know that this is somewhat below the market value, but are willing to sell at a discount to have a bulk sale.

What does this investment do for your IRA? Let's have another look at the numbers. If you add the sales price to three years of taxes, you come up with $401,700 in total expenses. ($390,000 + $11,700 = $401,700.) Divide this by your profit, and you get a return of 79.03 percent. ($401,700 ÷ $508,300 = 79.03 percent.) Divide this by the number of years you held the investment, and you find you have an annualized return of 26.34 percent. You might now be wondering if this can actually happen. Well, it did!

BUYING WITH LIMITED FUNDS

In all of the scenarios presented thus far in this chapter, the IRA account has contained sufficient funds to cover the real estate purchase. But what if you find a great piece of property—something that you and your crew firmly believe would be a valuable addition to your IRA—and your retirement account simply doesn't have adequate funds? Fortunately, there are a number of ways in which you can make the purchase and still keep the transaction both legal and profitable.

Loans

It is, in fact, possible to borrow money to buy property with your IRA. However, to do so legally, you must use the IRA-purchased property—not the IRA itself—as security for the loan. This is called a *nonrecourse loan*, meaning that if the loan isn't paid back as promised, the lender may take the IRA-owned property used to secure the debt, but may not take recourse against any other assets. If you are a homeowner, you will immediately see that this is very different from the loan you agreed to when you bought your home. If you fail to make payments on your home, the bank may not only foreclose, but, if necessary, may also attach your other assets—your car, for instance. Your IRA-related loan, on the other hand, can never affect any assets other than those used to secure the loan.

So now you know that you can get a loan to buy property with your IRA as long as only the property is used for security. The problem is that very few banks would ever loan your IRA nonrecourse money! So how can you obtain a loan with your IRA legally? Your IRA can get a private loan. For instance, the seller of the property can act as the bank, and you can pay him back just as you would have paid the bank. If the seller isn't interested in doing this, a friend, sibling, work associate, or nearly anyone else can make the loan, using either discretionary funds or their IRA. In any of these cases, you will have to fill out a promissory note, agree to a specific interest rate, and pay the lender back out of your IRA. And if you fail to make the monthly payments as agreed in the note, the lender will be able to foreclose. (See Chapter 5 for information about notes, and Chapter 7 to learn the ins and outs of investing with relatives.)

Easy, right? Well, a warning is in order at this point. This tactic should be used only if the annual contribution to your IRA and/or any income that your IRA receives will allow you to make the monthly payments on the loan. Consider a scenario in which you agree to buy a piece of property for $50,000, but your IRA is able to make a down payment of only $10,000. At 10 percent interest, your IRA would have monthly payments of $333.33 per month, or $4,000 per year. If your annual contribution limit is $3,000, you would not have enough cash flow to cover the deficit, unless you tapped other IRA resources. In simple terms, you would have more money going out than coming in, and that is not good. If you must borrow money to buy real estate with your IRA, do so only within your means. Of course, this is good advice not only when using IRA funds, but also when using discretionary funds.

Tenancy-in-Common Ownership

Eventually, you and your crew may find a piece of property that promises to build enormous IRA wealth, but that costs far more money than your IRA has to offer—or that your IRA can borrow. If this occurs, one possible solution may be *tenancy-in-common ownership*. In this form of ownership, each of two or more people has an undivided interest in the property, without the right to survivorship. In other words, upon each partner's death, his share will go to the person designated in his will rather than the other partners. Because each person's interest, or share, is undivided, each can sell his share at any time without the consent or agreement of the others.

How can tenancy-in-common ownership help you buy that must-have piece of real estate? Let's say that several of your friends or family members also want to invest in real estate with their IRAs. With a tenancy-in-common arrangement, you can buy the property together, with each person putting in the amount of money he or she has available. Each will own a certain percentage of the property. Then, as time goes on, each will get a proportionate share of the annual income and, ultimately, a share of the sale profits based on the ownership percentage.

Tenancy-in-common ownership also allows you to use both IRA funds and discretionary funds to buy a single investment. For instance, if your savings are adequate, you can buy part of the property with your savings, and part of it with your IRA. In another scenario, you can buy an interest in the desired property with your IRA, and friends and family can buy interests with their

Understanding the Steps in Buying Real Estate

You've just reviewed a property with your crew, and have decided that it would be a valuable investment to make with your IRA. What happens next? Whether you are buying a house, a commercial building, or a vacant lot, the process is essentially the same. If you are a homeowner, chances are that you know the basic steps involved. If not, this inset will acquaint you with the process.

■ The Written Offer

Let's start by stating that no verbal offer is binding. In some states, however, a written offer is a legally binding statement of the buyer's interest in purchasing a property, and when accepted, it binds the seller as well. Drafted and delivered by the buyer's real estate broker, it spells out all the basics, from the price that the buyer is willing to offer to the desired time frame for the purchase. The offer normally includes several contingency clauses. In other words, it stipulates that the sale will go through only if, for instance, financing is obtained and a number of repairs are made. In the best case scenario, the offer is made in the name of the IRA. If a self-directed IRA has not yet been set up, however, the buyer can make it in the name of any nondisqualified person (see page 130 for details), and list "and or assigns" next to his name. This will enable him to negotiate the transaction prior to sending it to the administrator for approval. In a pinch, the buyer can make it in his own name "and or assigns." It should be noted that in certain states, such as New York, a written offer is not legally binding.

■ The Period of Negotiation

Once the seller receives the buyer's offer, he may accept it, reject it, or make a counteroffer. If a counteroffer is made, the parties generally enter a period of negotiation, which can last anywhere from a matter of hours to a matter of weeks.

■ The Acceptance

Let's assume that, with or without negotiations, the offer is accepted. While this is good news, be aware that the deal has not yet been closed. At this point, both parties start working to meet the terms of the agreement. Inspections are performed; the title search is completed; repairs are made; financing, if any, is obtained; and all other steps are taken to satisfy the contract.

■ The Contract or Purchase Agreement

The contract—known by various names, such as the contract of sale, agreement of sale, and purchase agreement—is a legal document in which the buyer agrees to buy and the seller agrees to sell upon the mutually negotiated terms of the agreement. In addition to stating the sales price, the contract includes various other terms, such as the required condition of the property at the time of the closing. The contract is signed when the negotiations are over, as a prerequisite to the closing.

■ The Inspections

The buyer must make at least two inspections of the property. The initial inspection is made prior to negotiation for the purpose of determining any problems that need to be taken into consideration during the negotiation. The walk-through, which takes place shortly before the closing, gives the buyer an opportunity to inspect the property prior to taking possession. At this time, the buyer makes sure that the terms of the agreement have been met and that the condition of the property has not substantially changed since the previous inspection. (Note that if the buyer lives far from the property, the inspection can be made by his broker, by a company that specializes in inspections, or by another representative.)

■ The Closing

The closing is the event that transfers ownership from the seller to the buyer in accordance with the contract. When this is a formal meeting, as it is in states such as New York, it may be attended by the buyer and the seller, their attorneys, and the real estate broker. Closings can take place informally, as well, with the participants signing the papers at their convenience. At the closing, the contract of sale is amended if necessary, the buyer puts down the purchase money, the mortgage document is signed, and a new deed conveys the title of the property to the buyer. The documents are then recorded, and title passes. At the conclusion of the closing, the buyer's IRA legally owns the property.

As the above information hinted, the steps involved in buying property vary somewhat from region to region. Your real estate broker will be an invaluable guide during this process, and will make sure that everything is done in accordance with the laws of the appropriate state.

discretionary funds. The possibilities are endless—and totally legal. (To learn more about tenancy-in-common ownership, see the scenario on page 145 of Chapter 7.)

Limited Liability Companies

When your IRA doesn't provide sufficient funds for the purchase, and neither loans nor tenancy-in-common ownership provides a solution, another excellent option is the limited liability company, or LLC.

The *limited liability company* is a combination of a corporation and a partnership in which each party buys shares or membership interests in the LLC—which holds title to the property—according to the funds he has available. The term "limited liability" refers to the fact that like a corporation, the LLC limits personal liability to each of the parties involved, so that members cannot lose more money than they contributed. In other words, their other assets can never be touched. However, an LLC is taxed not like a corporation, but like a partnership, in that earnings are taxed only once, with the taxes being paid individually by the members.

Chapter 7 provides a scenario about using LLCs to make IRA investments with family members, and Chapter 9 is devoted to the LLC. For now, suffice it to say that the limited liability company can allow you to use your money in conjunction with the money of friends and family—as well as that of land developers—and buy properties ranging from small office buildings to sprawling shopping centers.

PAYING ANNUAL TAXES ON YOUR PROPERTY

You may think that when you buy property with your IRA, you don't have to pay any annual taxes on it. Unfortunately, you would be wrong. In all cases, you will have to pay property taxes. In some cases, you will also have to pay taxes on a portion of the income earned from the property.

First, let's look at property taxes, sometimes known as real estate taxes. If you're a homeowner, you're well aware that this annual tax charged by the government is based on the market value of your property. However, this tax is not the same everywhere in the country, but varies from county to county. Thus, a piece of property valued at $100,000 can result in annual property taxes ranging anywhere from $500 to $3,500. Naturally, because the property is owned by the IRA and the taxes are associated with an IRA asset, this tax must be paid with funds from your IRA. That's why it's so important to run the numbers by your trusty accountant before purchasing any real estate with your retirement account.

In addition, in accordance with Section 511 of the Internal Revenue Code, if your IRA-purchased property is mortgaged, or if a mortgage was incurred with its acquisition, you must pay annual taxes on any income produced. This tax, known as the *Unrelated Business Income Tax* (UBIT), was actually designed to affect the income of charitable organizations. It may therefore seem that the tax should not apply to IRAs. However, it does.

Since you are probably not familiar with the UBIT, let's look at it a little more closely. This tax, as you've already learned, does not apply to every property purchased with an IRA, but only to property that has related debt. So if you were able to pay cash for your retirement home or parking lot, you don't have to worry about the UBIT. In addition, your income is taxed only after deductions are made for expenses and for other items that are deductible in a commercial enterprise. Finally, the first $1,000 of your net income from the property is not subject to the tax at all.

A brief example should clarify the UBIT. Let's say that your IRA bought a house priced at $100,000. The down payment was $50,000, and your IRA is in debt for the remaining $50,000. Let's further assume that you were able to find a tenant for the house, and that after your annual deductions for expenses, etc., your IRA has a net income of $1,280. Since the first $1,000 is not subject to taxes, only $280 will be used in the UBIT calculation.

The amount of net income subject to the UBIT is determined by the relationship of the average amount of debt on the property during the preceding twelve months to the property's average *tax basis*—its purchase price, increased by improvements or decreased by depreciation—during the same period. In this case, the debt is 50 percent of the tax basis of the property. Therefore, $140—50 percent of the taxable net income—is subject to the UBIT. This amount is taxed at a trust tax rate—say, 37.5 percent. (The trust tax is a moving target, and is subject to change by the IRS with the approval of Congress.) So the tax for the year would be $52.50 ($140 × .375 = $52.50). Clearly, as the debt is reduced, the UBIT decreases proportionately.

RENTING YOUR PROPERTY

When real estate is purchased with an IRA, the most frequent "next step" is to rent the property out to cover the costs and, hopefully, to produce a nice income for the retirement account. Often, investors assume that their IRA administrator will manage the property for them. Administrators, however, will not take on this task. Moreover, some administrators will not allow you to manage the property owned by your IRA. Many other people, though, will be glad to manage the property for you.

If you, for any reason, are unable to manage your IRA-purchased property yourself, first consider hiring a professional property management company, which you can find in the Yellow

Pages or through an Internet search. Generally, these companies charge from 5 to 10 percent of the collected rent, depending on their specific duties. These duties can be limited to collecting the rent, or can also include paying the bills, cleaning and painting after a tenant leaves, and locating another tenant.

If the idea of hiring a management company doesn't appeal to you, think about hiring one of the professionals with whom you've been working. Your real estate broker would be a natural choice, for instance. He knows the property and may like the idea of profiting from all that work he's been doing for you. Another possibility is your brother—or any other relative who is not a disqualified person. (See page 130 for details.) This is a particularly good choice if your sibling lives relatively close to the investment property. And it will keep all the money in the family!

Considering all the money being paid *out* of your IRA account, for everything from taxes to management fees, you may now be wondering if it's possible to make a profit on your IRA investment. The following scenario should put your fears at rest.

Renting Property—A Scenario

Let's say that using your IRA, you have bought a condominium that will someday be your retirement home. The price of the condo was $100,000, and you made a down payment of $50,000. You obtained a loan for $50,000 at 8 percent interest, amortized over ten years. This will require a monthly payment of $418.22 per month. We'll estimate taxes and insurance at another $150 per month, and condo fees at another $100, giving your IRA a monthly negative of $668.22.

Clearly, it's time to get your condo rented so it can start paying the bills, and maybe even make some money. You know that you need a manager—someone to collect the rents and pay the bills—and the first person who comes to mind is your broker. He's done a lot of good work for you, and so far, you haven't paid him a penny. He's familiar with the property, which is a real plus. And you want to keep him in the loop for future investments. He thinks that this is a fine idea, and agrees to take on the job for $75 a month.

After placing an ad in the local paper, the broker finds a stable tenant with a secure income. She is willing to pay, and you are willing to accept, $850 per month. In addition, she will pay all utilities. You agree to renegotiate the rent every couple of years. You are now collecting $850, and are paying out $668.22 plus a stipend to your broker of $75. That leaves you with $106.78 extra every month, or about $1,280 per year. You have your retirement home of the future, and it's actually putting money back into your IRA. Does it get any better than this?

SELLING YOUR PROPERTY

Perhaps the only property you will ever buy with your IRA is your retirement home, and you intend to live there to the end of your life. However, if you choose to buy a number of different properties with your retirement fund, chances are, you will eventually sell one or more of them.

Selling property that was purchased with an IRA is much like selling property purchased with discretionary funds. You simply call up your real estate agent and tell him to put the house, commercial building, or whatever up for sale. In this case, of course, the proceeds will go not to you, but directly into your retirement account.

Will you have to pay capital gains tax on any profit made on the sale? If you made the original purchase of the property with a traditional IRA, you will eventually have to pay taxes on the gains, but not until you withdraw the money from your IRA after retirement. If you purchased the property with a Roth IRA, though, you will *never* have to pay taxes on your profit.

One more issue must be considered: The UBIT, or Unrelated Business Income Tax first discussed on page 75. That's right. If your property is subject to indebtedness, such as a mortgage, within twelve calendar months of the sale, the UBIT will come into play. The good news, though, is that the debt-to-tax basis ratio will have changed over time, so that your UBIT will probably not take a big chunk out of your profit. Moreover, because we're now discussing the gain made on the initial investment

78

rather than the income produced by the property, the UBIT will work somewhat differently. A brief example will clarify how the UBIT affects sales. Let's say that you bought a property for $100,000 and sold it for $200,000. Let's also assume that there was $50,000 debt on the property at the time of the sale—25 percent of the sales price. UBIT will then affect 25 percent of the gain, or $25,000. However, instead of the $25,000 being taxed at the usual UBIT rate, it will be taxed at a capital gains rate of around 20 percent, resulting in a tax of about $5,000. Not bad at all. (The exact rate of taxation will, of course, depend on a number of factors, such as the period of time for which the asset has been held.)

If the idea of paying taxes on your tax-exempt or tax-deferred investment bothers you, and if you have both the time and the means, simply pay the loan off twelve months prior to selling the property. (Since the IRS goes back twelve months in its calculation, you must pay off the loan prior to that date.) No debt, no UBIT.

Once you've sold a piece of property and your IRA funds are once again liquid, a host of options is available. You can immediately buy another piece of property; you can immediately make another real estate-related purchase, such as notes or options (see Chapters 5 and 6, respectively); or you can leave the money in your administrator's money market account until a good opportunity presents itself. And if you are age 59½ or over, you can withdraw the money from your account without penalty.

Selling Property—A Scenario

Let's say that eight years ago, you purchased a condo in a popular resort town with the idea of one day using it as a retirement home. The cost of the condo was $100,000, and you financed $50,000 of the price. Since then, you have been renting the condo out and using the resulting income to pay down the debt.

Now, however, your spouse is ill, and you decide that your condo is too far from necessary medical facilities. With much regret, you make a call to the broker, telling him to sell the property. You still owe about $10,000 on the original debt of $50,000.

Comparing IRA Investments With 1031 Investments

Many experienced real estate investors are familiar with Internal Revenue Code 1031, which allows individuals who hold property for trade or business—for the purpose of investment, in other words—to exchange one property for another without paying immediate taxes on the gain. As long as you continue to pyramid upwards, always buying more expensive property, you can avoid paying capital gains tax.

This concept of tax-deferred investing has been around for a long time and has been used by many to avoid paying taxes on real estate investments. Considering this option, you may wonder why you should use your IRA to purchase properties. Below, I have used a question-and-answer format to compare 1031 investments with IRA investments. You can be the judge of which choice provides the greatest benefits.

1. Is the tax on the gain deferred?
The tax on the gain for a 1031 property is deferred until you sell your last property.

The tax on the gain in traditional IRAs is deferred until you retire and start withdrawing money. Meanwhile, the contributions are tax-deductible. The tax on the gain in Roth and Education IRAs is exempt, meaning that you have already paid taxes on your contributions, and will never have to pay a capital gains tax. If your property is mortgaged or has other related debt, however, you will have to pay the Unrelated Business Income Tax. (To learn how this works, see page 78.)

2. Are there any rules limiting the people with whom you can do business?
The self-dealing rules on the 1031 say that you can't exchange real estate with members of your family. There are exceptions to this rule, but these exceptions require a longer holding period to qualify.

The self-dealing rules of the IRA say that your IRA cannot conduct business with you, your spouse, or your blood relatives. (See Chapter 7 for more information on disqualified persons.)

3. What is the effect of a cash sale?

If you sell your 1031 property for cash, you will immediately be taxed on your gain. One problem that often occurs at the time of the sale is a mortgage-over-tax-basis issue. If you have an investment that has a depreciable basis, such as an apartment building, the IRS allows you to depreciate the building over a period of years. It is meant to take into consideration that at some point in time, this building will deteriorate to the point that it is worthless. If you have reduced the adjusted basis through depreciation to a value below the existing mortgage, you will have mortgage-over-basis issues. When that happens, the amount of mortgage over basis is a taxable event, even though you did not receive the money. It is often referred to as phantom income. You show a gain on which you have to pay tax, but instead of that gain going in your pocket, it is used to pay down the mortgage. Hence, you have no money to pay the taxes.

When you sell your IRA property for cash, nothing happens. The taxable gain is either deferred or exempt, depending on the type of IRA you have—unless, of course, your property is mortgaged, in which case you will have to pay the UBIT.

4. Do you need to identify replacement property?

The 1031 requires that you identify replacement property for the exchange within 45 days of the closing of the transaction. Moreover, it must be like-kind property—which simply means that you must replace real estate with real estate.

The IRA does not require you to replace the sold property. If you never want to invest again, that's okay. If you want to invest in something totally unrelated, you can.

5. Must your replacement property have a higher price than your relinquished property?

A prerequisite of the 1031 is that the replacement property be more expensive than the relinquished property.

The IRA has no rule regarding the price of the replacement property. You are limited only by your imagination and your available funds.

6. If the property you sold or exchanged had a mortgage on it when you disposed of it, must the property you replace it with have debt as well?

Another requirement of the 1031 is that you must take on at least as much debt as you gave up. If not, you will be taxed on the difference in debt.

Not only don't you have to take on more debt with the IRA, you don't have to take on any debt.

7. Are there time frames for reinvestment of the proceeds?

IRC 1031 requires you to identify the replacement property within 45 days, and to close the transaction within 180 days or when you file your taxes for the year, whichever is sooner.

IRA rules provide no time frames for reinvesting.

The IRA is what I like to call a perpetual 1031, but with far fewer rules. This is not to say that the 1031 exchange is not a good way to conduct business outside the IRA. It is very effective and useful for the immediate avoidance of taxes. But the IRA provides much greater flexibility as you buy and sell your investment properties.

The good news is that the original projections made by your broker were correct. The $100,000 condo appreciated an average of 10 percent per year, and is now worth $215,000. When the broker sells the condo, your IRA will have made a tidy $115,000 in gain, all tax-deferred, right? Not quite. Remember that UBIT issue we discussed earlier? It's back. The good news is that the debt-to-tax basis relationship has changed, and is now only 4.65 percent ($10,000 debt ÷ $215,000 = .0465). So, if you take 4.65 percent of the gain ($115,000 × .0465 = $5,348.84), you end up with $5,348.84 subject to the UBIT. At a 20-percent capital gains rate, you owe only $1,069.76 in taxes. Not too bad for a $115,000 gain, is it?

In this chapter, you have learned how to select and purchase houses, lots, and even small commercial properties with your IRA. You have discovered that even when the funds in your IRA are not adequate to cover the cost of a property, it is often possible to buy the property and to enjoy a steady income from the purchase.

But not everyone wants or needs to purchase real estate as a means of building IRA wealth. Many other excellent investments are available. In the next chapter, you'll learn about the real estate-backed note—an investment that can provide both security and high returns.

5

Buying
Real Estate Notes

*A year's opportunities depend on the spring, a day's on
the dawn, a family's on harmony, a life's on industry.*

—CONFUCIUS, 500 B.C.E.

Qualified retirement plans have long used notes to receive
high returns. You can do the same with your self-directed
IRA and do so with little risk. The strategy is simple, and
can be quite rewarding if you know where to look and what professionals to use along the way.

This chapter begins by explaining what a note is, why it
makes such a secure investment, and what determines a note's
value. It then explains how you can originate a note by making
a direct loan—an option that will enable you to set every term
from the rate of interest to the length of the loan. Finally, you'll
learn the ins and outs of purchasing an existing note. Throughout, you'll discover how to keep your risk low and your returns
high, all the while adding to your IRA wealth.

Before you plunge into Chapter 5, it's important to understand that because this portion of the book is concerned with
low-risk investments, this chapter focuses on *first-position* or *senior* notes—notes that have no liens in front of them. These are the
most secure notes available. If you want to learn about higher-
risk, higher-return junior notes, see Chapter 8.

WHAT IS A NOTE?

If you are new to the world of real estate investment, a little background may be needed to bring you up to speed. Loans against real estate come in two parts: the security instrument, which may be a mortgage or a deed of trust, and the note. Most people know that when property is sold without full payment being made, the buyer signs a *mortgage* or *deed of trust*—a legal document that pledges the property to the lender of the money as security for payment. What, then, is a note? A *note,* sometimes called a *promissory note,* is a legal document that obligates the borrower to repay the mortgage loan at a stated interest rate during a specified period of time. The note, then, is essentially a promise to pay. It is what binds the borrower to the loan and the terms of the loan.

Promises to pay have been bought and sold for as long as real estate has been bought and sold. Banks sell their portfolios of notes regularly. The bank loans people money, creates a note and security instrument, packages it with similar loans, and sells the portfolio on the market. In order to make the investment attractive to buyers, the bank may discount the value of the notes slightly to increase the yield to the buyer. (More about this later in the chapter.) What I am going to recommend is that you buy these notes. But rather than buying portfolios for millions of dollars, you will buy individual notes in amounts that you can afford.

WHY BUY REAL ESTATE NOTES?

Why would you want to purchase a note instead of the real estate itself? No toilet to fix, for starters. When you purchase real estate, you have a responsibility to keep up the property to maintain your *equity*—that is, the value of the property over and above any debt incurred. If you let the property deteriorate, the value, as well as your equity, will deteriorate with it. Real estate ownership is an ongoing management concern. It can take constant work to maintain the maximum value of the property.

But when you own a note secured against real estate, it is the responsibility of someone else—the borrower—to maintain the property. He is responsible for fixing the toilet when it breaks. If he doesn't, he will lose his equity in the property. When you own a note rather than the property behind it, you also don't have to be concerned with finding good renters. That's the borrower's problem. There are no midnight calls saying that the roof is leaking.

Most investors come to me with the intention of owning real estate. But after we discuss the responsibilities that go with owning property versus owning notes, the majority chooses notes. Owning a note does not preclude you from owning real estate, of course; quite the contrary. If the borrower does not meet the obligations of the note, you may vary well become the owner of the property.

Here's why buying a note is so secure. The borrower has made a promise to pay you a certain amount, usually monthly. If the borrower fails to meet his promise, you will have the right to take his property away. That is called foreclosure. You will get the property, and the borrower's note will be forgiven. The borrower, of course, does not want that to happen. If it did, he would lose any equity he has in the property, get a serious ding in his credit, and probably have a taxable event. You see, the IRS looks at the relief of debt—in this case, the elimination of the note—as the equivalent of receiving cash. Therefore, the borrower would have to pay taxes on that phantom cash he did not receive. However, as the owner of the note, you will win whether or not the borrower is able to pay his debt.

WHAT DETERMINES A NOTE'S VALUE?

As you learned earlier in the chapter, a note specifies the amount of money to be repaid, the interest to be paid on the principal, and the period of time in which the debt will have to be satisfied. Naturally, each of these variables affects the value of the note. The value of the note also depends on the creditworthiness of the borrower. Finally, when buying an existing note, the price you pay—

which is not always the same as the amount of the loan—affects the value of the note. Let's look at each of these factors in turn.

The Amount to Be Repaid

The amount of money to be repaid must be considered in light of the value of the property. The relationship between these two elements is called the *loan-to-value ratio,* or *LTV.* A note with a lower loan-to-value ratio—in other words, a note in which the amount of money borrowed is smaller in relation to the property's value—is more desirable than a loan with a higher ratio. An example would be property with a value of $100,000 and a loan of either $40,000 (40-percent LTV) or $80,000 (80-percent LTV). Which LTV would make you feel more comfortable? The 40-percent LTV is a much more secure investment. Because the borrower has greater equity in this case, the borrower has more to lose and, therefore, more incentive to pay. And should you have to foreclose, you will pick up an additional $60,000 in equity, instead of the $20,000 you would receive with the $80,000 loan.

The Interest

The effect of the rate of interest on the note's value is clear: The higher the interest rate, the more valuable the note. But the type of interest being charged is also significant. Basically, there are two kinds of interest: simple and compound. *Simple interest,* which is the kind usually charged when making personal loans, is interest that's paid only on the *principal,* or the amount of the loan. For instance, if you loaned $300 to your sister for a year and charged her 1 percent interest, at the end of the year, she would pay you $3 in interest plus the principal of $300, for a total of $303. Simple interest—and compound interest as well—is always calculated on an annual basis.

Compound interest, which is the type charged by banks, is interest paid on both the principal and the accumulated interest of prior periods. If you loaned your sister $300 for one year but charged her 1 percent interest each day—in other words, if the interest were compounded daily—she would owe you $303 at the end of the first day, $306.03 at the end of the second day, and so on. As you see, if two notes have the same principal and the same interest rate, but the first charges simple interest and the second charges compound interest, the second note is of far greater value.

The Term of the Loan

Now, let's consider the period of time in which the debt has to be paid—the *term* of the loan. Aside from the basic truth that people would usually rather have their money back sooner than later, you must consider the fact that money received today is worth more than money received tomorrow. Why? Because of inflation, which averages 3 percent per year, the dollar weakens annually. Thus, the shorter the term of the loan, the more valuable the note.

The Borrower

Another determinant of value to consider when purchasing a note is the creditworthiness of the borrower. When you originate a loan—when you deal directly with the borrower, rather than buying an existing note—you have the opportunity to ask questions of the borrower. You can ask about his income, financial status, and credit. Obviously those individuals with a solid income, good financial status, and excellent credit are the best bets.

When you buy an existing note, you may or may not have access to this information. The original lender may not have delved into the credit of the borrower. And if he did, he may not share the results of his investigation with you. If the lender has no data to share, or if he refuses to share what he has, it is critical that you perform your own investigation of the note's history. Find out when the note was created, what its past payment history is, and what its current value is. How? The note itself will tell you when the document was created. The party from whom you are buying the note will be able to provide a payment history. And the value of the security can be determined through an appraisal of the property. Your real estate agent should be able to help you obtain this last piece of information.

If you're lucky, you'll be able to review the borrower's *credit report*—an evaluation of his history of debt repayment. Credit reports typically use an Empirica Score as a means of quantifying the borrower's ability to repay debt. My personal analysis of Empirica Scores is as follows: Scores of 800 and above are saintly. These people can be completely trusted to pay back their loans. Scores of 700 to 799 indicate good credit. Scores above 600 mean that you should consider the risk and weigh other factors. Scores of 500 to 599 mean that you should look at the property really closely—because you may very well end up owning it. How about scores under 500? If the borrower can explain the problems cited in the report, or if the loan-to-value ratio is very low, you still may want to buy the note. But be cautious.

Be aware that if you originate a note with a friend or relative, you can ask him to obtain a credit report and submit it for your review. A number of online services provide these reports free of charge. Just do a computer search for "Credit Reports."

The Price of the Note

When you originate a note, you invest the exact amount of the loan. When you purchase an existing note, however, you most commonly pay less than the amount that remains to be repaid. In other words, you buy the note at a discount. This, naturally, has the effect of boosting the value of the note. (To learn how discounting affects yield, see the inset on page 104.)

YOUR CREW

Whenever you are approached to lend funds from your IRA, you must remember that you are lending out the money you will use to pay for your retirement years. The decisions you make today will have a major impact on tomorrow. So go slowly, ask lots of questions, and seek advice. That's right: This is definitely a time you want to call in your crew.

Although it is usually not necessary to obtain help from a real estate broker when locating or buying notes, in some cases, a broker's assistance is valuable. If you are unsure of the value of the real estate that's securing the note, for instance, you'll definitely want to contact your broker. He will then be able to provide you with sale prices of comparable properties to help you evaluate the worth of the real estate.

If you are not comfortable analyzing cash flows, computing yields, and the like, you'll also want to call in your accountant. This is especially important if you are creating a note rather than buying an existing one. When originating a loan, you'll be able to negotiate the length of the loan, the size of the loan, and the interest rate. Your accountant can guide you in determining the most profitable terms.

If you are originating the note, your attorney will be needed to draw up both the note and the security agreement. If you are buying an existing note, you still may want to seek legal advice. If the note and security agreement are not straightforward, your attorney will be able to translate the legalese and identify any problematic clauses.

Although you will not be buying the real estate that backs the note, you must make sure that the owner has full title to the property and that this note will be in a senior position, meaning that there will be no liens before it. Therefore, you'll need your title insurance company to provide a title report as well as title insurance.

Working with notes necessitates the addition of a new crew member—a collection company, which will be responsible for collecting the note payments. Most IRA administrators require this, and if they don't, they usually charge an exorbitant fee for collecting the note for you. Title insurance companies and banks also can be used for this purpose at times. But over the years, I've found that the best collection companies are the stand-alone types, which can be found under "Collection" in the phone book. These companies collect the notes and use specialized systems to track the payments and notify both the borrower and the lender whenever the payment is late.

Finally, as in any purchase made with your retirement account, your IRA administrator will have to approve and fund the deal, and to file the appropriate paperwork with the IRS.

HOW DO YOU ACQUIRE NOTES?

There are two avenues you can take to acquire notes for your IRA. You can originate a note, or you can purchase an existing note. Let's look at each of these options.

Originating a Note

When you originate a note, you deal directly with the borrower and actually create the loan. Because the note is not already in existence, you have the opportunity to negotiate the conditions so that the amount of the loan, the interest rate, and the length of the loan are a good match for your resources, and promise both security and a healthy return. How do you go about finding an interested borrower? A number of possibilities are open to you.

Finding Opportunities to Originate a Note

The opportunities for lending money are vast. In fact, the popularity of capitalizing on cash flows has soared in the last ten years.

Perhaps in the past, you made loans to a friend in need of cash. Well, the same kind of loan can be made with your IRA funds, allowing you to help a friend and increase your IRA wealth at the same time. The scenario presented on page 94 will walk you through the process and, along the way, teach you how to construct a loan agreement that satisfies both the borrower's need for immediate cash and your own need for security and a solid return on your investment. Just keep in mind that when dealing with friends—or, for that matter, with any other party—the details of the transaction must clearly show that your primary objective is to make a good IRA investment, and not to help the other person involved. If this intention isn't clear, the IRS may deem the investment a prohibited transaction. (For more information on this, see page 132.)

You don't have a friend in need? Don't worry; there are many more ways to find a borrower. Mortgage brokers, also known as private moneylenders, can be found in every community. Go to them, introduce yourself, and tell them what you are attempting to do. Set your parameters and let them find the right opportunities for you. They work just like real estate brokers except that they're foraging for borrowers rather than property. When they find someone who seems like a good fit for you, they'll give you a call. And just like real estate brokers, they'll be paid by the borrower—not by you. Just keep in mind that even though these people are professionals, you should not assume that every deal they find is a good one. That's why the broker should provide a credit report on the potential borrower. If the supplied information doesn't satisfy you, ask for more. If you are still not satisfied, pass it up. There will always be another deal.

If you are more of a hands-on person, you can always call a couple of the larger real estate companies in your town and let them know that you have money to lend on real estate. You may be surprised by the response! Another way to find prospects is to put a simple advertisement in the newspaper. Most papers have a section titled "Money to Lend." If you choose to take the advertising route, though, be aware that you are likely to be contacted by some people who are very poor credit risks. Make sure to conduct a thorough credit search on anyone who responds to your ad.

Finally, you can get in touch with builders and developers. Every community has a builders/contractors association, which can be located in a number of ways. First, look for "builders/contractors associations" in your Yellow Pages. If this avenue leads to a dead end, the Internet may give you the information you seek. For instance, when I searched for "Washington home builders," I came up with several builders associations, including state and national groups. A search for "Washington real estate developers" yielded similar results. Finally, a well-informed real estate broker should be able to provide a name and number. However you find this information, give the association a call, and ask if it has a newspaper or trade magazine. If it does, place an ad. Soon, you will receive more responses than you ever wanted. Always in need of "opportunity" money, builders and developers typically identify an opportunity in their field and then try to secure the needed funding. Watch their credit, though; it's not always that great. The scenario on page 97 will guide you in working with builders and developers.

Creating a Note—Scenario 1

As discussed above, you may already know someone who would love to borrow money from you to fund a real estate purchase. And a note is the perfect way to provide your friend with the cash he needs, and you with a solid IRA investment.

Let's say that your friend has an opportunity to buy a parcel of land in Missouri for far less than the market price—if he can act quickly. The property is in the *path of progress*, meaning that development and industry are moving in that direction, and the property lies right in their path. Therefore, the property is sure to increase in value over the next few years.

Based on a current appraisal, the property is worth $130,000, but the owner is under duress and willing to sell it for $100,000 if your friend can give him the cash in the next ten days. Your friend suggests that you loan him half of the current value ($130,000), and he puts in the rest. You will be secured in first position on the land. This is important, as it means that in the event of foreclosure, you will be able to immediately take title to the property without first paying off other liens. In addition, your friend will pay you 10-percent interest on the borrowed $65,000 (50 percent of $130,000 = $65,000). He will pay the interest on a monthly basis, giving you $541.67 a month for two years. Then, when he sells the property, he will repay the principal. Note that while not all loans are structured as interest-only payments that end with a *balloon payment*—a final sum greater than those that preceded it—the vast majority of short-term loans do work this way. In addition, like most private loans, this one will charge simple rather than compound interest.

On the surface, this looks like a good deal. The loan has a 50-percent loan-to-value ratio, you have found a good borrower, and you have an appreciating property. It's just the type of loan one would want to make. However, some enhancements and changes could make this an even better investment.

First, consider the amount of the loan. The parcel of land has been appraised at $130,000 and the owner is willing to sell it for $100,000. If you took this type of deal to the bank—and if the bank would even consider making the loan—their response would be, "I'll loan you 50 percent of the appraised price or the sales price, whichever is less." The bank does that for a reason. The real value of any piece of property is the amount that a willing buyer will pay for it and a willing seller will accept—not the appraised value. The appraised value is just one person's opinion of the property's worth, and it can and often does prove to be wrong. In lieu of a bona fide sale, though, it is the bank's best resource for establishing value.

How can you improve the terms of the note? Offer to loan your friend $50,000 instead of $65,000. The lower amount will be equivalent to 50 percent of the sales price instead of 50 percent of the appraised value. What you don't want to do is get so buried in the property that a forced foreclosure and sale would not return your principal. An LTV of 50 percent is about as high as you want to go on vacant land.

Now, consider your friend's creditworthiness—a topic first discussed on page 89. You know your friend and believe that he will repay the loan. That's good enough for you. But what if in a year or so, you need cash and have to sell the note to raise money? To obtain a good offer, you will have to supply information on the borrower.

Fortunately, this problem is easily solved. Simply ask your friend to provide a credit report and a financial statement. The credit report, as mentioned earlier, can be obtained online. The financial statement, which can be written in longhand, should show his assets and liabilities. Alternatively, a form can be purchased at any office supply store. Then verify his income. You can do this with W-2 forms or payroll check stubs, or by getting his written authorization to contact his employer. This will provide the invaluable information that you will need should you ever want to sell the note.

Next, consider the interest rate. The 10-percent interest rate to which you've agreed may seem like a nice return at a time when banks have single-digit interest rates. However, you must understand that the reason your friend is approaching you, rather than a bank, is that this is a highly speculative loan—and banks don't like to make speculative loans. My experience is that anyone willing to loan money on unimproved land in the 50-percent LTV range charges at least 12-percent interest.

Again, the solution is fairly clear. Just raise the interest rate to 12 percent. The difference to your friend will be only $2,000 over the life of the loan—$6,000 in interest per year as opposed to $5,000 in interest per year. This will not be a make-or-break issue for him, and it will give you the return you are trying to maintain in your retirement account.

Now, consider the length of the loan. Your friend believes that this property will increase in value over the next few years. The implication is that at the end of two years, he will sell the property to pay back your loan. But two years isn't a very long time.

The solution? Give him a three-year loan. Never set a borrower up for failure. Nobody wins. He is going to need time to sell the property after realizing the appreciation. The rule of thumb is this: Add six months to a year to the time the borrower says he needs to repay the loan. Trust me; you don't want to have to go through foreclosure—with your friend or with anyone else—if it can be avoided.

Finally, consider your friend's assertion that your loan will be in first position. Is it true? Instead of wondering, request a title search and title insurance showing that there are no liens in front of your loan. Now you're not just sure. You're insured.

You've now adjusted the amount of the loan, the interest rate, and the duration of the loan, and you can feel confident that the monthly payments will safely increase your IRA for years to come. If circumstances change and you need your cash back more quickly, the credit report you requested will make it easy to sell the note on the open market. That is the beauty of investing in notes. They provide wonderful flexibility—flexibility that is not offered by all investments.

Creating a Note—Scenario 2

The previous scenario walked you through a fairly simple real estate investment. Not all, however, are so straightforward. Let's look at a situation that involves a land developer, and see the different ways in which this opportunity could be handled.

Let's say that you are approached by a small developer of residential building lots. His business is taking larger parcels of property, redesigning the property's lot lines, and adding the infrastructure—public works such as sewers and water systems— needed to make smaller lots for home construction. He has a ten-acre parcel of land that, through his expertise, he has turned into fifteen parcels. The project has been successful, and he has already sold ten of the fifteen lots for $40,000 each. His work is now done. The water and sewer lines, streets, curbs, gutters, and power are in, and builders are constructing houses. The developer is just waiting for the remaining five lots to sell.

The developer wants to move on. He has found another parcel that he wants to develop in the same way, but he lacks the money needed to acquire the new land. There are a couple of ways in which you can help the developer and yourself. First, you can finance the remaining five lots to give him the cash he needs for his new project. Second, you can finance his new development.

The first approach of financing the existing lots is probably the easiest. The retail value of the lots was already established by the ten earlier sales. In the previous scenario, I mentioned that a 50-percent LTV is about as high as you should go on vacant land. Land does not sell as quickly as property that includes buildings. You may have to reduce the price dramatically to sell it fast. That's why you want a fairly large cushion of equity above your loan.

The sale of the first ten lots has demonstrated that the retail value of the lots is $40,000 each. Therefore, having five of them gives the developer a value of $200,000. That means that a 50-percent LTV will produce a $100,000 loan. There are two ways to secure the $100,000 against the five lots. You can prepare five notes and security agreements—one for each lot. Or you can prepare one note and security instrument and place a *blanket mort-*

gage—a loan that covers more than one piece of property—on all five lots.

The blanket mortgage has definite advantages for both the developer and you. The developer will benefit because it costs less to draft one document than it does to draft five. But the blanket mortgage will benefit you most. When you put a blanket mortgage on the five lots, the developer is going to require that you put a release clause in the note so that if he sells one of the lots, he can pay a certain sum toward the principal, releasing the lot from the mortgage. So you have your attorney draft a release clause that allows the release of one lot when 125 percent of the principal attributed to that lot is paid. ($20,000 × 125 percent = $25,000.) Here comes the advantage: By the time the fourth lot is released, the loan will have been paid back. You see, the last thing you want to do is be fully involved in the very last lot in the subdivision. That is obviously the least desirable of the lots, and will be the hardest to sell.

You also instruct your attorney to add a clause stipulating that you will receive a minimum of six months interest no matter when the money is repaid. How would you feel if you went through all of this work to provide the loan funds, and one week after the closing, the developer sold all of his lots to a builder and paid off your loan? Your IRA would have garnered a measly $231 for your effort. You must make sure that you are providing for your retirement, and you can't do that by loaning your money out for a week or two at a time—not at 12-percent interest. With the six-month guarantee, you know that your IRA will be increased by at least $6,000 for your efforts.

Now, let's consider the second scenario, in which you finance the developer's new project. At this point, it's important to understand that at each stage of development, land has a different value. First, there is the value of the raw land—land that has no improvements such as sewer systems. This value is essentially the amount that the developer pays for the land—$100,000, for instance. Then, there is the second stage, when the developer has taken the property through the planning and zoning process and has obtained preliminary approval from the governing authorities to break the land into several parcels. Usually, this approval has several conditions attached: creating a green area, bringing in sewer and water lines, and the like. This preliminary work adds value to the property—say another $100,000, for a wholesale value of $200,000. Finally, there is the completed or retail value of the individual lots. This may add another $100,000 to the entire parcel for a total value of $300,000.

Let's say that the developer makes a $100,000 offer on the raw property for his new project, subject to getting preliminary approval on the property in a specific period of time. If he is unable to obtain that approval, the contract to purchase is void. He pays for the engineering costs and consulting costs to get the property ready for preliminary approval, which gives him a vested interest in the property. In other words, if he doesn't finish this project, he is going to lose money. You offer to loan him the $100,000 at the time he receives preliminary approval. If he gets the approval, you give him the loan. You now have the 50-percent LTV you wanted, and he can satisfy his purchase agreement. The development goes forward. As in the previous scenario in which you funded the first development, you have your attorney include a 125-percent release clause in the note, as well as a clause stating that you will receive a minimum of six months of interest no matter when the loan is repaid. The developer pays you out of the sale of the lots. Just make sure to have your attorney read the preliminary approval to verify that the conditions applied by planning and zoning are not so restrictive as to damage the profitability of the development.

Creating a Note—Scenario 3

So far, we've looked only at loans made against unimproved property—raw land and land that has been subdivided into lots. But you can also originate notes on improved property. A little more work is involved when the property includes structures. One problem is that it is often more difficult to place a value on a house than it is to establish a value for a lot. Another is that while a lot can't burn down, a structure can. But, as you'll see, each of these problems has a simple solution.

Let's say that that one of your coworkers tells you that he has a need for cash, and that he wishes to use the rental house he owns as security. He wants to borrow $100,000. The value of the property, he states, is $250,000.

The loan he suggests would create a 40-percent loan-to-value ratio, which is sufficiently low. However, when you call the county assessors office, you find that on the tax rolls, the property is valued at only $175,000. While this sends up a red flag, you know that it is not unusual for the assessed value to be lower than the actual value of the property. You call your real estate broker and ask him to prepare a list of comparable sales. He finds three similar properties that recently sold for an average of $240,000. This makes the loan-to-value ratio about 42 percent, which is still acceptable.

Naturally, you ask the borrower to provide a current credit report. He complies, and his credit checks out. You also hire an inspection firm to make sure that the structure is sound. So far, you're good to go.

You're glad that the house is a rental, because that means that there will be no restrictions on the amount of interest charged on the loan. Some states have laws that prevent you from charging over a specified rate of interest for loans on a primary dwelling. Naturally, you have no intention of charging a usurious interest rate, but you do want to choose a rate that will give you a fair return on your loan. Since a rental is considered commercial rather than residential, the state laws should not prove to be a problem.

You decide to loan the money for 12-percent interest, which will be calculated on an annual basis, and paid in monthly interest-only payments of $1,000 for three years. The principal of $100,000 will be repaid at the end of the third year.

You contact a title company and ask that a preliminary title report be drawn up along with a note and deed of trust (a mortgage). The title report comes back showing that there is already a first deed of trust secured against the property in the amount of $25,000. When you question the borrower, he states that it was a loan from a family member, and that $25,000 of your loan will be used to pay it off immediately. This will put your note in first position, making it far more secure than it would be if it were junior to the first loan.

Earlier, I mentioned that when a note is backed by improved property, you must make sure that you're protected against loss of the structure. Knowing this, at the closing, you have yourself named as an additional insured on the insurance policy in the amount of the loan. This means that if the house burns down or is otherwise destroyed, you will be the first to receive money when the proceeds are paid. Now you know that your investment is truly secure.

Purchasing an Existing Note

Many times, the lender who originated a note would rather have his money today than receive payments over time. He therefore seeks to sell his interest in the note. The holder of a note can sell it at any time he wishes—right after creating the note, or many years later. Of course, as time goes on and payments are made on the loan, the *note balance* changes—that is, the actual amount of principal that remains owed. Sometimes, a note is sold at its current balance. Sometimes, the interest rate is so high and the term is so short that the seller is actually able to charge more than its current balance. Most commonly, however, notes are sold at a *discount*—that is, at less than their current balance. Banks do this for a number of reasons. Sometimes they are low on available cash, and have to liquidate notes for ready money. Sometimes they have the opportunity to put the recovered cash to work on a more profitable investment. Whatever the reason, the discounted note offers a great opportunity to the savvy investor, who can often obtain high returns while enjoying a secure investment. (To learn more about this, see the inset "Understanding the Yield of Discounted Notes" on page 104.)

Buying a Discounted Note—A Scenario

You now know a little bit about the purchase of discounted notes. The following story—an actual example from Captain Miles' account—will show just how you can use discounted notes to build IRA wealth.

As you may remember from Chapter 1, my goal with Captain Miles was to obtain rapid asset growth in his IRA. I therefore searched for a note that had a strong likelihood of providing the jumps in yield discussed in the inset on page 104. I wanted to find improved property—specifically, a rented house. You see, home-owners within the United States typically sell their homes every five or six years; owners of rental properties sell every three or four years. Our odds for an early payoff would be better with a rental house—especially if the owner had already held the prop-erty for two or three years.

A real estate broker offered just the type of opportunity I was looking for. The broker explained that the note was on a rental house in Bloomington, Indiana. The owner of the note had placed it on the market because he needed money to buy another prop-erty that he desperately wanted. The condition of the purchase dictated that he sell his note to obtain the needed cash by the fif-teenth of the month. If he could meet that deadline, he would sell. If not, both deals would be off.

Several of the broker's points piqued my interest. The loan was only 50 percent of the current market value; the property was a rental house that the current owner had owned for several years; and the owner had just finished remodeling—an improvement that would increase the property's value as soon as it was record-ed on the tax rolls. Moreover, the seller of the note needed money quickly to take advantage of another investment. This was one of those truly special investments that you have to move on quickly.

My first job, I knew, was to verify the information provided by the broker. A contact in Indiana steered me to a Bloomington broker who set about inspecting the property. Next, I called an attorney in Bloomington to discuss foreclosure laws and any com-plications we might expect should the mortgage go into default.

The next day, the broker's report indicated that the property had a value even higher than previously thought. This is not unusual. When selling notes secured by real estate, sellers often rely on the value of the property when it was last sold. When it comes to investment returns, however, *today's* value is what is important.

I had ordered a preliminary title report immediately upon making the offer on the note. Copies were sent both to me and to the attorney in Bloomington. His call three days later confirmed that the title was clear of defects. He reported that in the unlikely event of foreclosure, there should not be any delays or extra costs.

With the title report reviewed and the value of the property confirmed, I turned to the note and mortgage. The mortgage secured a ten-year note that was three years old. The remaining balance owed on the note was $34,353 and was payable monthly at $307.15, including 10 percent annual interest. There would be a balloon payment in seven more years of $31,823.

Due to the seller's eagerness for cash, I made an offer that was fairly low—$20,000 for the $34,353 note. I was somewhat surprised when the seller came back with a quick affirmative response. He could have raised more money by shopping around, but he had a rapidly approaching deadline, and the $20,000 was enough to cover his next investment.

The attorney in Bloomington set up a collection account at a local bank, notified the mortgagee that the payments would now go to that collection account, completed and assigned the mortgage to The Captain's IRA, and named the IRA as an additional insured on the liability and fire insurance policy. With that done, we closed the deal. All of this took less than a week.

The property proved to be a truly exceptional investment. The discount we had applied to the purchase of the note already guaranteed over $14,000 more than what we paid ($34,353 - $20,000 = $14,353). The original note stipulated an annual interest rate of 10 percent, which, when combined with the discount, created an annual yield of 22.04 percent—if the note paid exactly as scheduled. Of course, it did not, which is what we were counting on.

As explained earlier, we had good reason to expect an early payoff. Only nine months after The Captain's IRA purchased the note, the property was sold and the new buyers obtained new financing—which paid off the old loan. The remaining balance at that time was $34,159. After investing only $20,000, the IRA had

Understanding the Yield of Discounted Notes

To appreciate the benefit of discounted notes, it's first necessary to understand that interest and yield are not always the same. Technically, the interest rate is the percentage used to determine the charge for borrowed money. The yield is the interest or return earned on an investment. Sometimes the yield is the same as the interest rate, and sometimes it's not. To understand why, let's look at a few notes and see how different variables affect the yield.

Let's say that you buy a ten-year note that was originated by a bank. The note balance is $10,000, the interest rate is 10 percent, and payments of principal and interest will be made in monthly installments, which is typical of bank loans. Because such a note yields compound interest—interest not just on the principal but also on any unpaid accumulated interest—each monthly installment will be $132.15. Therefore, if this note pays as agreed, over the life of the contract, you will receive your $10,000 investment back plus interest in the amount of $5,858. Your investment will be worth $15,858 at the end of the ten years—a yield of 10 percent each year.

Now let's see what happens when the same note is purchased at a discount—for less than the current note balance of $10,000. Let's

received nine payments equaling $2,764 *and* the principal balance of $34,159. The annualized rate of return was a whopping 88.03 percent. The Captain's IRA had increased in value from $20,000 to $36,923 in less than a year!

ORIGINATING VS. PURCHASING NOTES

At this point, you may be wondering what the major differences are between buying an existing note and creating a new one. The differences can be summed up in two words: *profit* and *risk*. When you originate a note, you can negotiate the various terms to your say that the holder of the note is in need of immediate cash, and is willing to take less than the current balance to receive it. You offer and he accepts $8,000 for the note. You are now going to receive ten years of monthly payments of $132.15, which will give you the same $15,858 as before. The difference is that now you will also receive $2,000 more than your original investment. So you will have a gain of $7,858 instead of $5,858. Your yield will now be 15.63 percent per year.

Now, let's take it a step further. This time, you not only purchase the note for $8,000 but, for one reason or another, the borrower pays the note off early—say, at the end of the third year instead of the tenth year. So after receiving $132.15 monthly for three years, you receive the balance of the original note—$7,960.32—$2,000 of which you did not pay for. You are, in essence, receiving your $2,000 discount seven years earlier than expected. You now enjoy a 19.70-percent yield on the $8,000 you invested. Here's another way to look at it: $5,960.32 is the principal return, and the discounted $2,000 is the interest.

As you can see, the yield of an investment is determined by more than just the interest rate. Other variables include the price paid for the note, when and how the payments are made, and early payoffs. These factors can boost the yield far above the interest rate, making the discounted note a truly outstanding IRA investment.

liking, minimizing risk. In addition, you can thoroughly investigate the borrower, and can choose one who is truly creditworthy.

The same cannot be said of purchasing an existing note. When you buy a note, you cannot negotiate terms that reduce risk; you have to accept existing terms. Moreover, you often have to base your judgment of the borrower solely on his payment record for that particular note. On the other hand, because of these factors, and because the holder of the note is often desperate to sell, it is often possible to buy an existing note at a discount. The result, of course, is a higher profit. Moreover, as long as you stick to buying senior (first-position) notes with low to moderate loan-to-value ratios, your risk will be relatively low. If the borrower fails to make payments, you will always have the option of foreclosure. While this may not be your preferred outcome, it will help insure that your principal is returned to you.

Notes secured against real estate are a solid investment offering a range of returns, from modest monthly gains to truly staggering yields. Plus, they are wonderfully flexible. You can keep the notes until they are paid off or, if you need immediate cash for a more lucrative investment, you can sell them on the open market.

But notes are not the only way to build your IRA through real estate. In the next chapter, you'll learn about an array of less traditional real estate investments that can yield high returns while keeping your retirement money safe.

Nontraditional Real Estate Investments

When one door closes, another door opens; but we so often look so long and so regretfully upon the closed door, that we do not see the ones which open for us.

—ALEXANDER GRAHAM BELL (1847–1922)

So far, we have discussed traditional types of real estate investments—buying property, and buying notes secured by property. In this chapter, you'll learn about a number of nontraditional investments for your IRA, including options, tax sale certificates, foreclosure sales, and judgments. Some of these investments, such as options, are easy to find, and are already building IRA wealth for many savvy investors. Others, such as judgments, may require a bit more sleuthing on the part of you and your crew. All of these investments, however, are relatively low in risk and can yield high returns for your retirement account.

THE OPTION

For the purpose of this discussion, an *option* is a written, recordable right to purchase a property under certain terms and conditions, within a specified period of time. The difference between an option and a contract of sale (purchase agreement) is that options allow you to back out of the purchase without consequence—

other than losing whatever money, known as *option consideration*, you have paid to that point. A purchase agreement does not.

Here's another way to look at the difference between an outright purchase and an option. If you purchase property, you have full rights to use it in any way that is available according to the law. You own it; it's yours. The option does not give you those rights. The original owner retains the property rights, subject to any conditions of the option. But the option does give you the exclusive right to purchase the property at the previously agreed-on terms, or to sell the option itself to someone else. And no one—not even the owner of the property—can legally sell that property without first satisfying your option. To put it another way, you can control the sale of the property until the option expires—that is, as long as you make the payments. If you fail to make the payments or if you do not exercise your option to purchase, all of the rights revert to the owner.

Why Buy an Option?

Why would you buy an option rather than simply buying the real estate itself? An option may be a good choice for a number of reasons. Perhaps your IRA doesn't have cash available to purchase the real estate. Perhaps you don't have time for due diligence—a careful study of the property and its predicted investment performance. Perhaps before the purchase, you need to enhance the property in some way to create more value. Or perhaps you think you have found a "hot" piece of property, but you won't know for sure for a year or so. Whatever the reason, options will add to your IRA wealth as long as you find real estate that you can option for a low price and sell at a higher price. And in most cases, while the property is appreciating in value, the owner of the property—not you—will keep paying all of the inherent costs of the property, including taxes, assessments, and maintenance.

Your Crew

Once you decide to invest in options, you'll want to gather your crew. First and foremost, you'll need your real estate broker to find opportunities and to thoroughly research each option property. If your broker cannot provide market research showing that there is a reasonable chance that the property will substantially increase in value during the option period, don't option it! Always remember that options are for selling, not holding. Your ultimate goal is to sell the option to somebody else for a profit.

Should you involve your accountant in the option-buying process? This decision should depend on the complexity of the transaction, and on your own ability to perform the necessary calculations. If you feel comfortable doing this work yourself, you may be able to avoid paying an extra fee. If not, definitely give your accountant a call.

Your attorney will be responsible for drawing up the option agreement and having it filed at the county courthouse. You want to be on record at the county courthouse as having an option so that the property cannot be sold without notice being given to you. As long as this document is on file, your option will hold. If the property is sold with title insurance and the title company overlooks the recorded option, the title company will have to pay the buyer back through his insurance policy.

I can't overemphasize the importance of using your title insurance company. No real estate transaction—whether it be a purchase, an option, a lease, or a loan—should be completed without first reviewing the preliminary title report and ultimately obtaining title insurance. Just because the owner of the property believes that it is unencumbered doesn't make it so. Liens and other obstructions could have been placed on the property without his knowledge. Get the title insurance, and know that your investment is a safe one.

As is true of every IRA investment, all of the paperwork will ultimately be sent to your IRA administrator. The administrator will then approve of the deal and fund it through a wire transfer made directly from your account to the closing agent, who may be either your attorney or a title company. The administrator will also be responsible for filing all of the appropriate paperwork with the IRS.

Buying an Option—Scenario 1

The story of a simple short-term option will clearly show how options can help you build your IRA. Assume that your real estate broker calls you one afternoon explaining that he has a "hot deal." He has just heard that a major wholesale club is coming to your area, and that it is considering a parcel of land just outside of town for its building site. This is one of the reasons you are using a broker; because he is in the business of real estate, he is the first to hear of deals like this. This "hot" plot is the only parcel that fits the club's needs, and it's just a matter of time before the company's corporate office makes an offer. In addition, there is a five-acre parcel adjacent to the identified parcel that is also for sale, and has been for three or four years. The owner of the property, unaware that the club is on the way, is ready to sell. Until now, there hasn't been a real market for either parcel.

The adjacent parcel of land is for sale for $3,000 per acre, but your broker tells you that the only comparable values he has found in the area justify a sales price of $2,500 per acre. If the sale to the club takes place, the value of the ground will soar to $10,000 per acre or more! Why? This is now *path of progress* land—property toward which development and industry are moving. The wholesale club will draw peripheral businesses that complement the club.

Immediately, you pick up the phone, call your attorney, and have him draw up an option to purchase the land at the full asking price. This is not a time to quibble; the deal may disappear if the owner or another investor gets wind of the impending deal. You option to purchase the land for three years, with the option consideration—the money you must pay—being $2,000 per year. In other words, by giving the seller $2,000 per year, you will own the right to purchase the land for three years at a value of $15,000 ($3,000 per acre × 5 acres). The three years of option payments will reduce the principal amount by $6,000 ($2,000 × 3 years = $6,000), so at the end of three years, you will owe only $9,000 if you exercise your option to buy ($15,000 − 6,000 = $9,000).

The owner readily accepts your offer. Why? Well, for starters, he will not be required to pay taxes on the option payments until the option to buy is exercised, so he will be able to use the option money tax-free for up to three years. He may also anticipate being in a lower tax bracket by the time of the sale, which means that he can actually save money by selling the property at a later time, when his taxes are lower. Moreover, the option has increased his chances of selling a property that has had questionable market value for the past several years. And, of course, he's just received an offer that is $500 per acre more than the market value of the parcel.

One of the beauties of this option is that you won't have to do anything to enhance the value of the land. All you'll have to do is wait until the club's store is built, and the value of the adjacent land goes up. Another benefit is that you were able to gain control of the property with only $2,000. Had you purchased it instead of optioning it, you would have had $15,000 tied up in the land. If the club's deal went south, you may have been left holding a parcel of ground for some time before you could recover your investment. The fact is that you will probably know in the first year whether the club is going to build. If the deal falls apart and you don't see an advantage in continuing your option, you can simply fail to make your second-year option payment. It won't affect your credit. You will have simply lost $2,000 on your investment. The seller will have benefited by way of any option payments he has received, and will be free to sell or option to someone else. Life will go on.

Suppose, though, that the wholesale club does go forward with its plan. A few months after you obtain the option, the deal closes, and the company starts breaking ground almost immediately. Because of the way they fast-track these buildings, with cities and counties bending over backwards to get them up and running, the store opens for business shortly after you make your second option payment. The market value of your option is increasing rapidly. In fact, it is becoming so attractive that the owner asks if he can buy the option back from you. Your response is an emphatic "No!"

Around the end of year two, the market value of your option has reached $50,000. You have had several inquiries, and now it is time to sell. What do you have to sell? You don't own the real estate, but you do own the *option* to buy the real estate. If someone else buys your option, he or she can then purchase the five acres for $11,000 ($15,000 less two payments). Therefore, your equity in the option is now $39,000 ($50,000 sales price less $11,000 owed). So you sell your option for $39,000, and the option's new owner has to pay the owner of the land the $11,000 still owed on the original option. You have turned $4,000 into $39,000 in two years. Moreover, to do so, you put only $4,000 at risk instead of the whole $15,000. Not bad at all.

It should now be clear that an option—backed by good due diligence on the part of your broker—is a great way to build your IRA. Could you make this same investment with discretionary funds—savings, in other words? Yes, but if you did, you would have to pay taxes on the entire gain. In other words, the investment would be fully taxed. If you buy the option through a traditional IRA, however, you will pay taxes only when withdrawing the money at retirement, making the investment tax-deferred. And if you make the investment through a Roth IRA, you will *never* be taxed on the gain.

Before we leave this scenario, let's change it a bit to highlight the benefits of the option. Let's say that instead of purchasing an option to buy the land, you purchased the land itself. If you put $2,000 down on the land and had the owner carry back a loan of $13,000 for ten years, with 10-percent interest and a balloon payment at the end of year three, you would pay about $171.79 per month, or $2,062 per year. Over the three-year holding period, that would total $6,186. Add that to your down payment of $2,000, and you would invest $8,186 and be on the hook for $13,000 more. Of the $6,186 in payments, $3,533 would go to interest. So by purchasing the land, you would increase the amount you pay—or decrease your profit—by $3,533, and you would increase your liability from $2,000 to $15,000!

Buying an Option—Scenario 2

The first scenario I presented was for a short-term option, but there are times when a long-term option is viable.

Let's say that friends or non-blood relatives are living on a fixed income—an income fixed by the government, and fixed far too low. The only asset they own is their house, but they don't want to sell it because they've lived there all their lives and want to continue doing so. They don't want a mortgage because they are afraid that if they miss a payment, the bank will take the house back. Besides, with their income, who would loan them money?

You have your real estate broker verify the value of your friends' house at $100,000, and offer to option their property at $500 per month, with the payments reducing the principal amount. You state in the option agreement that the owner will have a *life estate* in the property, meaning that he and his spouse can continue to live there for the remainder of their lives. Upon their death, or if the owner decides to vacate the property due to poor health or for other reasons, you must exercise your option to purchase within six months. You are not concerned about how long your friends will live because it is a nice house, they take good care of it, and it will continue to increase in value with time. Should you die before the homeowners, the option will pass to your estate or to the beneficiary of your IRA.

Your friends will enjoy the benefit of receiving $500 per month tax-free for the rest of their lives, or until they decide to vacate the property. Why tax-free? An option is taxed only when exercised, and it will not be exercised until the death of the owner. Should your friends die prior to the option's being paid in full, there will still be some benefit to their heirs. The value of the house at death has already been established at $100,000, so the heirs will not have to pay for an appraisal. Plus, the estate will have cash to wind up its affairs because you are required to pay the remaining option amount in cash to the estate within six months of death. It is true that the kids won't get the current value of the house at the time of death, but that is not what this option is all about. It's designed to provide for the owner and spouse during their lifetime, not to leave a big inheritance for the kids.

What will be the benefits to your IRA? You just bought an investment for no money down—an investment on which you'll *never* have to pay interest. When was the last time you got a deal like that? True, you can't receive rent from the investment until the owners vacate the property, but the appreciation on the property—as well as the fact that you are paying no interest—should be return enough. If the prevailing interest rate was 8 percent and the appreciation factor was 6 percent, you would get a 14-percent return on your invested dollar. Not bad.

Buying an Option—Scenario 3

In the preceding scenarios, the option was structured so that you would have to do nothing to maintain or improve the property until the option was exercised. However, options can be structured so that—both for your benefit and that of the owner—your improvement of the property is actually a condition of the option agreement.

Let's say that you ask your real estate broker to hunt for property in the path of progress. Moreover, you specify that the property must have certain characteristics. First of all, you want it to have been for sale for a while, a circumstance that usually makes the seller a little more malleable. Second, you need the property to have an opportunity for "upside"—a term which indicates that the property can be made to appreciate in value through an increase in rents, renovations, rezoning, a change in neighborhood patterns, or natural but significant growth.

The broker drops everything and starts the search. He does this because he knows that you are a closer. You have completed several deals with him, and he respects your ability to make decisions and act quickly with your IRA funds. In no time at all, he brings you a wonderfully ugly commercial property that fits the bill. Located in Ames, Iowa, the property is a vacant lot that's covered with abandoned cars and other rubbish. Sitting in an old section of Ames that has long been neglected and forgotten, the lot, as well as most of the property around it, has been for sale for years. That takes care of any questions about the compliancy of the seller.

The upside of the property is twofold. First, a new bond levy has been passed by the city to bring sewer and water lines to the area in an effort to improve the neighborhood. The area is just now being served with these utilities. In addition, the city and neighborhood representatives are in the process of funding a downtown growth study. This will determine what needs to be done to make the once-vital area thrive.

The second factor that offers an upside is that a new freeway will be built through the area, and an off-ramp may be constructed adjacent to the lot. This has been in the works for years, and has finally been funded by the Federal Government. The owner is well aware that sewer and water lines are coming and that there may be an off-ramp some day, but he has been frustrated with this lot for years, and is eager to hear your offer.

Any property sold in the area has commanded a price of about $1 per square foot. Since the lot is slightly more than two acres in size—about 90,000 square feet—it would be expected to sell for $90,000. Because of the opportunities lurking on the horizon, the owner wants $120,000 for the property. But after some negotiation, he agrees to $90,000. Why? You explain that as a condition of your option, you will clean and level the lot, and will bring in water and sewer lines. If you fail to make these improvements, you will lose the option. The owner is well aware that the sewer and water lines will cost in the neighborhood of $20,000, and no one knows what the cleanup might cost. Plus, you explain the advantages of taking taxed-deferred option money instead of making a fully taxable sale. These benefits, along with the anticipation of having his lot cleaned and improved, make the owner willing to negotiate.

Because of the costs needed to improve the property, you offer to pay the owner $10,000 in option consideration in year one, $20,000 in year two, and $30,000 in year three. The remaining $30,000 will be paid if and when you choose to exercise the option. You have staggered the amounts of the option payments because you realize that the value of the property will be increasing each year. Therefore, you will feel comfortable putting up larger amounts as time goes by. If you don't buy the property within the three-year period stipulated in the agreement, you will lose what you have thus far invested. Why are you willing to pay so much money for this option? Very simply, because the seller is aware of the proposed off-ramp, he is going to require larger payments. In addition, your broker's due diligence has shown that a ready-to-build lot is worth about $2 per square foot. The investment, therefore, is a solid one.

After your IRA puts up the $10,000 due the first year, and the deal is closed, you quickly hire a contractor to clean the lot and install the water and sewer lines. The total cost of this work is $25,000. You now have $35,000 at risk—$25,000 to the contractor and the $10,000 option consideration. But at this point, the property is worth $180,000, and your IRA has an option to buy it for only $80,000 more. So far, so good. A year or so goes by, and the construction of the freeway off-ramp is finally approved. Business is picking up in the area, and you get three offers on your property from speculators who just want to buy and hold the lot until the ramp comes in. The $200,000 they offer looks good, but unlike the owner of the property, you are not desperate. You wait.

The third year comes. It is time to fish or cut bait. In order to keep the option active, you are going to have to come up with $30,000. You and your broker consider the situation, and you decide to go for it. Your IRA pays the money, and you have your broker start actively marketing the property at $6 per square foot. The off-ramp is finished, and the option on the property sells. Your IRA paid, with costs, a total of $115,000 for the property—$90,000 option consideration plus $25,000 to the contractor—and not one penny went to interest. Your IRA then sold the property for $540,000. Your retirement account just increased by $425,000 in three years. If you used a Roth IRA, that money will be available to you tax-free at retirement.

Right now, you may be questioning whether this was truly a low-risk investment. Despite the relatively large amount of money involved, it definitely was low in risk because of the excellent due diligence performed by the broker. It is impossible to overstate the importance of your broker thoroughly researching any option property. In this scenario, the broker determined that the off-ramp was a near certainty. He also determined that a $25,000 cleanup would double the value of the property, making it worth $180,000 in the first year. Always remember that you are putting your retirement money at risk, and that good information is of paramount importance. Also keep in mind that even though you can eliminate *most* of the risk, you can never eliminate risk entirely.

TAX SALE CERTIFICATES

In a number of states, when the owner of real estate is delinquent in paying his property taxes, the county or other taxing unit sells its right to foreclose in the form of *tax sale certificates.* These certificates give the buyer the right to collect lawful interest; to give proper notices to foreclose; to obtain possession of the property by court eviction; and to reside in, lease, rent, or dispose of the property at will. The taxing authority offers the certificates at a discount in order to raise money quickly and avoid the hassle of foreclosure. The owner of the property still has the opportunity to redeem his property by paying the overdue taxes plus the interest and any penalties. A call to your tax assessor will determine if you have the opportunity to buy certificates in the state in which you live.

Why Buy a Tax Sale Certificate?

The tax sale certificate offers a great opportunity for those who are just starting out with their IRAs. The purchase prices on these liens are often in the hundreds of dollars, rather than the thousands. When you have small amounts to invest, you traditionally have to rely on lower-yielding investments. But with the tax sale certificate, returns can be relatively high—sometimes as high as 18 to 20 percent per year. If you purchase two or three of these certificates a year, you can increase your IRA very quickly.

While returns on tax sale certificates can be high, the biggest growth in your retirement account will occur when the property owner does *not* redeem his property by paying overdue taxes. In this case, you will end up owning the property for pennies on the dollar. This means that you will either get a good return on your investment or a great one, without any real risk.

Are there any disadvantages to buying tax sale certificates? It takes a lot of work to keep reinvesting the monies as the tax liens pay off, and the downtime between investments can significantly reduce your annual yield. These investments also require a good deal of work from your IRA administrator, who may charge you a little more than usual for his services.

Your Crew

To a large extent, you will sail this boat alone. However, two crew members will be needed onboard.

You will not require your broker to locate tax sales. You'll be able to do that by contacting the taxing authority and following the directions they provide. However, once you find a promising piece of property on which taxes are due, you'll want to determine its value. And for a small fee, your broker will be able to check comparable sales and make sure that the real estate is worth the investment.

Your trusty IRA administrator has to be involved in every IRA investment, of course. In the case of tax sale certificates, you will send the paperwork provided by the taxing authority to your administrator along with a direction letter, which will instruct the administrator to write the check directly to the county or other authority. The certificate will then be sent directly to your administrator. If the owner of the real estate pays his taxes, they will be paid to your IRA, and the administrator will release the lien. If foreclosure is necessary, your retirement account will receive the title to the property.

Buying a Tax Sale Certificate—A Scenario

Because the available funds in your retirement account are relatively low, you decide that a tax sale certificate would be a smart investment. An Internet search provides you with the phone number of your county's taxing authority, and you give him a call to learn when the next tax lien sale will take place. He not only provides the date and time of the sale, but also directs you to a website that lists the delinquent properties.

The site, you find, lists literally hundreds of properties. You're like a kid in a candy store. Which to choose? You could, of course, buy a few properties sight unseen in the hopes that a number of them will end in foreclosure. But you know better than to gamble with your retirement money. Therefore, you pick out a property that looks good to you, as the taxpayer is several years behind in payments and the property is worth far more than the taxes. Then you contact your broker and ask him to research the investment.

The real estate in question is actually four tax lots of five acres each, for a total of twenty acres. It is carried on the tax rolls with an assessed value of $2,000 per acre, or $40,000 total. However, the broker's investigation shows that the land around it has been selling for close to $3,000 per acre. The taxes owed are $1,500 per lot, for a total of $6,000. You take the time to inspect the property, and find it to your liking. You wouldn't mind owning it.

Although the auction won't take place for another week or so, you contact your IRA administrator and direct him to fund an escrow account in the amount that you're willing to bid on the liens. Your research has shown that the taxing authority wants to be paid sometime between immediately and forty-eight hours after the sale. Therefore, you have to have the money available.

The day of the auction arrives, and you're ready. You show up at the courthouse steps, where you are given a bid number on a card. As it turns out, the very first property to be called out is the one in which you're interested. You have learned that the auction values in your state are based on the yield of the tax lien. In this case, the minimum yield is 16 percent. This means that once a taxpayer is delinquent, he must pay the amount of the taxes plus 16-percent annualized simple interest. So, if, for example, the taxing authority can sell the lien at a 10-percent yield, it will have picked up the tax ($1,500 per lot) plus 6-percent interest. The other 10 percent will go to the buyer of the lien.

The bidding starts, and you offer 16 percent. Someone else offers 15 percent. You get the bid at 14 percent. This means that you will pay $6,000 for the tax sale certificate, and the taxpayer must give you $6,000 plus annualized 14-percent interest to redeem the lien.

In this case, the owner of the property is both willing and able to pay his delinquent taxes. Eighteen months after your IRA buys the lien, the taxpayer redeems it. Now the $6,000 goes back into your IRA along with eighteen months of interest, or $1,260. ($6,000 $\times$ 14 percent = $840 $\div$ 12 = 70 $\times$ 18 months = $1,260.) Your IRA has increased in value from $6,000 to $7,260.

What would have happened if the property owner had not redeemed his lien? In most counties, three years of delinquencies must take place before you are allowed to foreclose. This would mean that you would have to pay taxes for two more years to maintain your position. Because you paid the first year's taxes, the county would give you priority in purchasing these next two years. So after three years of payments, you would have put $18,000 into your investment ($6,000 $\times$ 3 =$18,000). You would then foreclose and, assuming that the property had not appreciated in value over the last couple of years, you would end up with a $60,000 piece of property for $18,000. This would give your IRA a whopping 110-percent annualized return.

FORECLOSURE SALES

When the owner of real estate fails to make payments on his mortgage, the bank—or whatever other institution or person holds the mortgage—goes through the foreclosure process, in which the owner is deprived of the right to redeem the mortgaged property. This is followed by a *foreclosure sale,* which is the public sale of the mortgaged property. Proceeds of the sale are used to repay the debt, with any excess going to the mortgagor.

Over the years, I have seen the popularity of foreclosure sales ebb and flow. There are times when you can go to a foreclosure sale and be the only one in attendance. There are other times when the sale is attended by hundreds.

It works like this. Usually every week, at a specified date and time, the sheriff stands on the courthouse steps and calls out the sale of foreclosed properties. Any bidders present may offer whatever they want for the property. Typically, the mortgage holders will be there and will bid the amount of what is owed to them.

Check your local newspapers to find out which properties are being foreclosed. All foreclosures must, by law, be posted in the paper for a required period of time—which varies by state—prior to the sale.

Why Buy a Foreclosed Property?

Foreclosure sales have always been an opportunity waiting to happen. Because mortgage holders are eager to receive the money owed to them, they are usually willing to accept a price that is far below the property's market value. This means that you can often purchase real estate for an amount that is quite small relative to its true worth. In most cases, the goal is to turn around and sell the property for a far higher price. Another strategy is to use the property as an income-producing rental.

On the downside, it takes a good deal of work to invest in foreclosures. You have to find the properties that are being foreclosed and, when you locate one that you are capable of buying, you must perform all the research necessary to determine its true value. Many properties are foreclosed because the amount of the mortgage is greater than the worth of the property. Naturally, you don't want to bid on those.

Your Crew

You'll probably want to begin your search for a good investment by contacting your real estate broker. As mentioned earlier, you can learn of foreclosures through your newspaper. You also can develop a relationship with your banker and have him alert you to foreclosed properties. But your real estate broker is in an excellent position to ferret out the best foreclosed properties for you. The only problem is that unless you pay him a fee, he may not be too agreeable to helping. To get around that, sign an official buyer's/broker's agreement that states that if he presents a property to you and you buy it, you will pay him a commission. In return, he will conduct the search and perform all the due diligence on the properties. If the broker does all of the work, he *deserves* a commission. Even if you find the property yourself, you will still need your broker's expertise to help establish the property's value. He can also help you determine the chances of leasing the property after acquisition—if that is your goal. Remember that you don't want to purchase just any foreclosed property. You want one that will provide a nice return for your retirement account.

If you are comfortable crunching the numbers, and if the property you're considering has simple income and expense streams, you may be able to make the investment without consulting your accountant. But if the income and expense streams are relatively complicated, by all means, contact your accountant. His expert advice will be well worth the price.

You may or may not need your attorney to assist you in buying foreclosed properties. In some states, the title company will draw the deed to convey title to your IRA. If this is not the case, you will need the services of your lawyer.

You title insurance company will, of course, be used to complete a title search and provide insurance. When buying a foreclosed property, you want to make sure that the property is free and clear of any liens.

Finally, your IRA administrator will be at the ready to approve of the deal, provide the funding, and file the appropriate paperwork with the IRS.

Buying a Foreclosed Property—A Scenario

One evening, while scanning your local newspaper, you notice that a house is being foreclosed in your area. Recognizing an opportunity to build your IRA, you note the trustee's name and number, and decide to give him a call.

The next day, the trustee refers you to the bank that holds the mortgage on the house. When contacted, the bank sends you a complete package on the property, including specifics such as house size, lot size, age, and more. In addition, the bank provides figures on the foreclosure. The bank had loaned the borrower $125,000, which he has since paid down to $98,000. But the borrower has missed the last ten payments of $917 each, and legal fees have accrued to the tune of $1,600. This means that the bank will be bidding around $108,770 at the auction. ($917 × 10 = $9,170. $9,170 + $1,600 + $98,000 = $108,770.) This is important information, as the bank will be your main competition.

On your way home from work, you drive by the house and notice a for-sale sign in the yard. This is not unusual. The owner is trying to sell the house before the foreclosure so that he can get something out of the property. If the house is foreclosed, the owner will probably lose everything. You call the agency listed on the sign, and are advised that the asking price is $175,000. This price is puzzling to you, but the agent explains that the asking price is based on solid market value. Moreover, the seller is trying to pay off certain debts, and if he doesn't receive his price, he will simply let the house go back to the bank.

Now you call in your real estate broker and have him provide a list of comparable sales. He finds that the market value of the house is truly $175,000. This is good news. Your only worry is that the house will be sold by the owner prior to foreclosure. Of course, you would never pay the asking price because you are only interested in making a profit on the property—not in using the house as a residence. You decide that you would be willing to pay $125,000 for the property. Why? First, you have that amount of money available in your IRA, making it a viable purchase. Second, you feel that a $50,000 profit would be very nice, giving you a 40-percent return—as long as you can resell the house for $175,000, of course. In fact, with that kind of cushion, you can reduce the price if necessary and still enjoy a handsome return.

You contact your IRA administrator and have him place $125,000 in an escrow account, ready for the transaction. On the day of the sheriff's sale, you go to the county courthouse. There, the lender bids $110,000 and you bid $115,000. Because there are no other bidders, the property is yours. A sales contract is executed with the county. You pay $115,000 from your escrow account and send the remaining $10,000 back to your IRA. If you are able to resell the house for anything close to its market value, your IRA will enjoy a welcome growth spurt.

JUDGMENTS

A *judgment* is the decision of a court in a civil action, stating that one individual is indebted to another, and fixing the amount of the debt. For instance, if a renter fails to pay rent, the landlord can obtain a judgment from the court against the renter. Judgments are generally secured against all of a debtor's assets, including his real estate. To build your IRA, you want to focus on buying judgments that are secured against property that is of sufficient value. A judgment will not give you the right to foreclose on the property. However, when the property sells, you will be the first creditor to be paid. And, of course, the judgment debtor—the person against whom the decree has been issued—may be able to repay the judgment without selling the property that's involved.

Why Buy a Judgment?

You don't see judgments offered on the open market very often, but when you do, you'll often find high profit margins. It's important to understand that a judgment causes an interruption in the life of the judgment debtor. He can no longer sell a piece of property without the judgment showing up against the title. Every time he applies for a loan, the judgment appears, and the judgment will be senior to any new loan he obtains. Obviously, lenders don't want to see that. Therefore, the judgment debtor usually has to pay the judgment, which means a payoff for you. The only question is: *When* will it be paid?

Because of the inability to predict when the debtor will pay the judgment, a heavy discount is usually applied to its purchase. Judgments can sometimes be bought for as little as 25 cents on the dollar. Couple this with the fact that judgments come in all sizes, both large and small, and you have an investment suitable even for those whose IRA funds are relatively low.

Your Crew

This is one of those rare cases when you *won't* contact your real estate broker to find an investment. Instead, you'll want to contact your attorney, who is in a better position to hear about judgments, and can also assist you in determining whether a judgment has value. An even better choice would be a good litigation lawyer. If you or your attorney knows one, tell him that you're in the market for judgments so that he'll be on the watch for good opportunities. As already mentioned, judgments are not offered on the market very often. Moreover, very few investors actively seek them out. But when they are available, they often make excellent investments.

Although your real estate broker won't be the first crew member to bring onboard, you'll want to give him a call if you have any doubts about the value of the property against which the judgment is secured. His resources will allow him to easily determine the property's worth.

As is so often true, the decision to call in your accountant should be based on your own ability to perform the necessary calculations. If you feel comfortable doing this work yourself, by all means, handle it solo. If not, though, don't hesitate to call for help.

While title insurance is not available for this type of transaction, you'll want to review the title on the property held by the debtor. This will help you determine if the judgment has been properly recorded.

By now, you know that every investment you make with your IRA must involve the administrator of your retirement account. Your IRA administrator must approve of the project, provide the funding, and make sure that the IRS receives all the necessary documentation.

Buying a Judgment—A Scenario

You have decided that a judgment would make a good addition to your IRA investments. Although you have advised your attorney of your interest, you also scan the legal notices of your local paper, looking for an opportunity. There, you find that a judgment has been issued against a construction company in the amount of $100,000. The judgment will be secured against the assets of the company.

When you contact your attorney with this news, he does some investigating and finds that this may not be a judgment you want to pursue. It seems that the judgment is attached to the construction company only, and not to the principals involved. "What's wrong with that?" you ask. Well, the construction company has few assets, and because of the lien, it will be restricted from doing business as usual. The attorney feels that because of these circumstances, the collection of the judgment has been seriously jeopardized.

The good news is that your attorney has found another judgment. This one is for $70,000, and is against a sole proprietor of a business. In this case, the judgment is secured not just against the business, but also against the proprietor—which means that it's secured against all of the proprietor's real property as well. Your attorney feels that even though the proprietor has been reluctant to pay the judgment, he will eventually have to do so. As always, the question is *when?*

Your attorney has performed his research well, and has found that the business owner is very active in the real estate market, and has also made plans to expand his business. Because the judgment will seriously restrict the proprietor's ability to obtain loans, your attorney estimates that the judgment will be paid off in five years at the most. Due to the uncertainty regarding the time of payment, a discount is in order.

You're definitely interested in this judgment. So, as the next step, your attorney contacts the holder of the judgment—the individual who stands to receive the promised funds. He indeed wants to sell the judgment. In fact, he has an immediate use for the funds.

You call your real estate broker, who, after some research, is able to assure you that the business owner has sufficient equity in his property to secure the judgment. Meanwhile, you have handed the numbers over to your accountant, who calculates that if it takes five years to collect the judgment, you can offer $33,220 and maintain a 15-percent annual return. A 10-precent return would require an investment of $42,545. After consulting with your attorney regarding the creditor's motivation, you decide to offer

$40,000, which will give you an annual return of 11.25 percent based on a five-year return. The creditor accepts, and the deal is completed.

What would happen if the debtor surprised you by paying the judgment off in four years? You would receive a 14-percent return. Three years? Your return would be 18.8 percent. Two years? Your return would be 28.3 percent. And if the judgment was paid in one year, your return would be 57.3 percent. In the worst case scenario, you would have a good return. In the best, a spectacular return. And you can do it all through a low-risk investment.

You have now learned about a wide range of investments. So far, though, most of the investments we've discussed have involved only you as the investor. In fact, an earlier chapter highlighted the fact that government rules prohibit your IRA from doing business with your spouse or with certain blood relatives and their spouses. There are, however, perfectly legal ways to involve family members in a variety of IRA transactions, further building both your retirement wealth and theirs. Chapter 7 will show you how it's done.

IRA Investments and Family Members

Call it a clan, call it a network, call it a tribe, call it a family.
Whatever you call it, whoever you are, you need one.

—JANE HOWARD (1935–1996)

Many IRA holders have at one time or another attempted to loan money to a family-member-in-need only to be told by their administrators that family members are the forbidden fruit of the IRA. To bite into that apple would certainly cause one to run afoul of the IRS. Some administrators don't think that the IRA can make *any* loans to *anyone*.

The fact is that you can not only make a loan with your IRA, but you can make it to certain relatives—as long as the investment makes good financial sense. You can also rent IRA-purchased property to relatives, providing reliable tenants for yourself while helping out your family. Moreover, you can join your IRA with those of relatives and buy real estate that provides everyone with healthy returns. This chapter will guide you through these investments, giving you more ways to build IRA wealth.

WHAT YOU CAN AND CAN'T DO WITH YOUR IRA

Many people limit their IRA investments to only the most traditional forms—certificates of deposit, for instance—for fear of making a prohibited transaction and incurring the wrath of the Internal Revenue Service. While it's true that prohibited transactions should be carefully avoided, it's also important to understand that as long as the transaction is not with a disqualified person and not a specifically prohibited transaction, it's a perfectly acceptable investment.

Earlier in the book, I mentioned some prohibited transactions. But now that we're discussing the option of making IRA investments with members of your family—an area that scares many if not most investors—it's vital to understand exactly what causes a transaction to be deemed prohibited. There are three parts to a prohibited transaction, and all three elements must be in place to make the transaction forbidden. First, the transaction must take place as part of your IRA retirement plan, including traditional IRAs, Roth IRAs, Education IRAs, Keogh plans, SIMPLE IRAs, and SEP-IRAs. Second, the transaction must involve a disqualified person, which you'll learn more about a little later in this chapter. And third, there must be a transaction between a disqualified person and the plan. (You'll also learn about this later in the chapter.) *Without the presence of all three, you do not have a prohibited transaction.*

Clearly, all of the transactions we're talking about in this book are made with funds from your IRA, so the first condition described above is in place. Let's take a look at the other two conditions and learn exactly what may and may not be done with your IRA.

Which People Are Disqualified From Making Transactions With Your IRA?

I will start by putting a myth to bed. It simply isn't true that you can't loan money from your IRA to relatives—or that you can't make other IRA investments that include relatives. Internal Revenue Code Section 4975, paragraph (c) (1) states that you cannot make IRA transactions with your "spouse, ancestors, lineal descendants, and spouses of lineal descendants." Moreover, it states that this applies not only to *your* spouse, ancestors, etc., but also to those of anyone involved in the administration of the plan—for instance, the spouses of involved administrators, trustees, and investment advisors.

What, exactly, does this mean? It means that you can't make any IRA investments with your husband or wife or with anyone in the bloodline directly above or below you: your natural parents, your natural grandparents, and your natural children and their spouses. Moreover, you can't make any IRA investments with your adoptive parents or your adopted children, because in the eyes of the law, they are the same as blood relatives. And as stated earlier, you cannot make IRA investments with anyone involved in the administration of your plan, or with their spouse or blood relatives. Who's left? Your brothers and sisters, your spouse's brothers and sisters, your spouse's parents, your spouse's grandparents, your grandparent's spouse (if not your natural grandparent), your stepchildren, your spouse's stepchildren, your aunts and uncles, and your cousins. (For a fast look at "who's out" and "who's in"—the people with whom you can't and can make IRA investments—see Table 7.1 on page 132.)

For some of you, this information alone is worth the price of this book. You probably had no idea that you could help family members with your IRA. And, of course, you can also rent property to relatives and even make IRA investments with relatives. But before we go on to the many ways in which your IRA investments can include family members, let's learn which specific investments are prohibited.

What Transactions Are Prohibited?

Now you know which people are considered disqualified. Additionally, it's important to avoid types of transactions that have specifically been prohibited by Internal Revenue Codes. These prohibited actions are as follows:

❏ Your IRA cannot do business with any disqualified person. While some investors try to find loopholes, years of experience have taught me this important fact: If someone is on the list of

TABLE 7.1. WITH WHOM CAN YOU MAKE IRA INVESTMENTS?	
WHO'S OUT	**WHO'S IN**
You	Your brothers and sisters
Your spouse	Your spouse's brothers and sisters
Your natural parents and/or your adoptive parents	Your spouse's parents
Your natural grandparents	Your spouse's grandparents
Your natural children and/or your adopted children	Your stepchildren
The spouses of your natural children	Your spouse's stepchildren
Any fiduciary of your IRA—such as an employee of the company that serves as your IRA administrator—as well as his spouse, ancestors, and descendants.	Your grandparent's spouse, if not your natural grandparent
Any people providing services to your IRA—such as your stockbroker—as well as his employees and both his and his employees' blood relatives.	Your aunts, uncles, and cousins

disqualified people (see "Who's Out" in Table 7.1), you cannot make any IRA investments that involve their doing business with your IRA.

❏ You cannot use your IRA funds in an investment whose primary purpose is to benefit you or another party—whether a total stranger, a friend, or a qualified or disqualified relative—rather than your IRA. To put it another way, the primary purpose of any IRA investment must be the enhancement of your Individual Retirement Account. If the IRS deems that a party other than the account is receiving an undue benefit, it can rule that you have a prohibited transaction. For example, if you give your brother an unsecured loan from your IRA with an interest rate of 2 percent when the market rate for such a loan is 9 percent, the government could deem the transaction prohibited. While you may have an ulterior motive to help out a friend or relative, the details of the transaction should not reflect that this was your primary objective over and above making a good investment for your retirement account.

❏ As a participant in your Individual Retirement Account, you cannot borrow money from your IRA, nor can you borrow money against an asset that is owned by your IRA. Moreover, you cannot assign or pledge assets of your IRA to another person. However, in any twelve-month period, you can make a withdrawal of any amount from your IRA as long as you roll that exact amount back into your IRA within sixty days. If not, the loan will be counted as a distribution, and you may be penalized, typically by 10 percent. In addition, if you have a Roth account, you may be taxed on top of that according to your tax bracket.

❏ You cannot use your IRA funds to make a loan to a corporation, including a limited liability company and a limited partnership, when 50 percent or more of the stock ownership in that company is held by you or by another disqualified person— your spouse, your parents, or your children, for instance—or by any combination of disqualified persons.

❏ You cannot purchase life insurance with your IRA.

❏ If your IRA is an employee benefit plan such as a SEP-IRA or a SIMPLE plan, and more than one employee is involved, you are subject to the Prudent Investor Rule. This rule states that before making an investment, you must consider alternative investments that are similar to the one being considered, and choose the best investment in terms of return and risk. If you make an investment despite the fact that another one is obviously better in terms of having less risk and higher returns, you will be subject to the wrath of the IRS. However, since most IRAs are not employee benefit plans, this is not a concern for the vast majority of IRA investors. Moreover, if you are the only employee involved in a SEP or SIMPLE plan, the Prudent Investor Rule doesn't apply to you.

❏ You cannot use your IRA to invest in any property considered to be a collectible by the IRS. This property includes, but is not limited to, the following:

- Works of art

- Rugs or antiques

- Metals or gems

- Stamps or coins

- Alcoholic beverages

How Do These Rules Work in Action?

You now know about the people who are disqualified from making IRA transactions with you, and you're familiar with prohibited investments. But as you might remember from the beginning of this chapter, there are three parts to a prohibited transaction: it must take place as part of your IRA, it must involve a disqualified person, and there must be a prohibited transaction between the disqualified party and the plan. To understand how these rules work in action, let's consider the following examples.

Let's assume that you purchased a house with your IRA, and then rented it to your daughter. Does this scenario include all the elements of a prohibited transaction? Well, first, you are using an IRA, so the first element is there. Second, it involves a disqualified person—your daughter. Finally, the transaction is definitely taking place between a disqualified party and the plan. Therefore, you have a prohibited transaction.

Let's try another scenario. In this one, let's assume that your IRA buys a 40-percent interest in a limited liability company (LLC). (You'll learn more about LLCs later in the chapter.) Your mother also invests in the LLC, buying a 20-percent interest. Is this transaction prohibited? First, you are, again, using your IRA, so that element is there. Second, it does involve a disqualified person—in this case, your mother. But do you have a transaction between a disqualified person and your IRA? No! The transaction is between your IRA and the LLC, and your mother and the LLC. Therefore, it is not a prohibited transaction.

Now, let's take the second scenario a step further. Suppose that the LLC gets into financial trouble and needs money, so it goes to its members for a loan. Your mother then decides to loan the money to the LLC. Is this transaction prohibited, or is it the same as the one above? This transaction is, in fact, prohibited, because it is between your mom, who is a disqualified person, and the entire LLC and its members—including your IRA.

Keep in mind that this section on prohibited IRA investments has not covered every possible investment that may be prohibited by the IRS, but was designed to make you aware that there are restrictions on your IRA investments. That's why whenever you make nontraditional investments, it's an excellent idea to call on the expertise of your accountant or attorney. Starting on page 229, you'll find a complete copy of the most important codes that regulate IRA investments, as well as an Internet site that provides access to all IRA-related codes. Show these to the appropriate members of your crew so that they'll be able to better guide you as you build IRA wealth.

LOANING MONEY TO RELATIVES

As you learned earlier in the chapter, it is perfectly permissible to use your IRA to loan money to certain relatives. Not only are these loans legal, but they can help your IRA grow. Consider the following scenarios, both of which involve the use of notes. (For detailed information on investing in notes backed by real estate, see Chapter 5.)

Loaning Money to Relatives—Scenario 1

Let's say that your brother comes to you in need of help. His company was recently downsized, causing him to lose his job. He is behind in his mortgage payments, and the bank is about to foreclose on his house. Although your brother has some good employment prospects, it may be awhile before he gets back on his feet. In the meantime, no bank will loan him money because he is unemployed.

You know that your brother will rebound. He had a good education and works hard, so it will just be a matter of time before he finds another job. What to do? First of all, if you have adequate savings, I strongly suggest that you lend him money out of your discretionary funds. Why? Because even though this is your brother and you would trust him with your life, it's a high-risk loan. That's why the bank won't make it.

If your savings aren't adequate, though, you can have your IRA loan him money. Assuming that your brother has equity in his home, my first recommendation is to loan him the money on a promissory note secured by his property, as described in Chapter 5. Yes, you will be in second position, but being secured is better than not being secured. Remember that if your brother doesn't find work, he may have to declare bankruptcy at some point. Then, if you are a secured creditor, you will have a much better chance of recovering your money, as the asset that you are secured against could be sold by the court, with the proceeds of the sale going first to the creditors secured by that asset.

Of course, you can choose to loan your IRA money directly to your brother on an unsecured promissory note. That will mean that your brother owes money to your IRA, and that only his sig-nature backs the promissory note. But, as mentioned above, this will place you in a precarious position. You see, the unsecured creditor in a bankruptcy is thrown into a pot with all of the other unsecured creditors. If there is any money left over after the pay-ment of the secured creditors, the funds are divided among all of the unsecured creditors. That means that in the best of situations, you would probably get only pennies on the dollar. This is not to say that you would have no recourse. You could always go to court and file for a judgment against your brother and any secu-rity he owns. But this is a long and complicated process, and not one you would undertake lightly. Moreover, not all self-directed administrators make unsecured loans. Remember that we're talk-ing about money that's earmarked for your retirement, and that you should never take any loans made with your IRA lightly.

Now that you've been frightened into the first choice, how should you proceed? Gather your crew. Yes, even when dealing with relatives, you need to make sure that everything is done cor-rectly. So do yourself, your family, and your IRA a favor and make it legal. Furthermore, in accordance with an earlier discussion in the chapter (see page 132), make sure that the details of the transaction show that your primary objective is to benefit your IRA—not to help your brother. (For more tips on avoiding pitfalls when making investments with relatives, see page 150.)

As described in Chapter 5, have your attorney prepare the documents. He needs to prepare a promissory note and security instrument—a mortgage or deed of trust. In this case, the security instrument will be recorded by the title company in second position behind the bank's note. That means that if the property has to be sold, the bank will get paid first and you will get paid second. The title insurance company will provide title insurance, just as if this transaction did not involve family members. If there are any questions regarding the value of the property, have your real estate broker prepare a comparative market analysis. This should cost you very little, and will give you great peace of mind.

Loaning Money to Relatives—Scenario 2

If you can originate a note to loan money to your brother from your IRA, it stands to reason that you can purchase a note from him, as well.

Let's assume that your brother is in the trouble discussed in Scenario 1. Let's further assume that several years ago, he sold a home and carried back the paper on the home himself. In other words, the buyer gave your brother a $20,000 down payment on the house, as well as a note for the $60,000 balance of the purchase price. The note and security instruments are in a first-position lien on the house your brother sold.

The note was structured to pay out over thirty years at an interest rate of 7 percent. That provides a payment of $399.18 per month. Although your brother has this income, it is not adequate to solve his current problems.

Your brother's borrowers have been diligent in their payments, and after four years, $57,285 remain to be paid on the note. As a means of solving his financial problem, your brother has taken the note to a couple of mortgage brokers to see what they would pay for it. The best offer he received was $33,298. That discount would give the mortgage broker a 14-percent yield. Your brother comes to you and tells you of his woes. You mention to him that you would be pleased to have a 10-percent return if you could buy the note with your IRA. And you can! You calculate that a 10-percent yield would give your brother $44,305 instead of the $33,298 offered by the mortgage broker. That would mean a $399.18 payment per month to your IRA, and a balloon payment at the end of the term.

Because you are a little unsure of your ability to calculate yields, you call your accountant. Accountants often can give you calculations over the phone. All they need to know is the original balance of the loan, the date of origination, and the interest rate or payment amount. Your accountant confirms your figures. You then have your attorney draw an assignment of the security instrument and send it to the title insurance company for recording. Your attorney also has your brother endorse the note over to your IRA. You fill out the necessary direction letters for your self-directed administrator, and the paperwork is done. You have a nice note in your IRA, and you've helped your brother over a rough spot.

You might ask why the mortgage broker would offer only $33,298 for the note. Why would he demand such a high yield? Remember that this is his business. He makes a living by buying notes and selling them to the public. Think of the difference between selling your car to your neighbor and selling it to a car dealership. The dealership has to make money on your car to stay in business. Your neighbor does not. Therefore, your neighbor can pay more for your car.

RENTING PROPERTY TO RELATIVES

Your investments with your relatives don't have to be limited to notes backed by real estate. As long as you stick to the rules and deal only with those family members approved of by the IRS code, you can also rent IRA-purchased property to relatives—and use the resulting monthly income to beef up your retirement account. Let's see how this can work. (For details on buying and renting property with your IRA, see Chapter 4.)

Renting Property to Relatives—A Scenario

Let's say that you're planning to buy a retirement home in Albuquerque, New Mexico. You want to retire there because that's where your spouse's children reside, and you and your spouse want to spend your retirement years near his kids and their kids—your grandchildren. Since the residence is for your retirement, you purchase it with your IRA. But rather than rent it out to a stranger and risk having a bad tenant, you decide to rent it to your stepson and his wife. They need a place to live, and you know that they will take care of your home and maintain your equity in the property.

You make it perfectly clear to your stepson that you are merely renting this house to him—that when you retire, it is your intention to make it your own home. Your real estate broker finds a modest house that fits your needs—it's on a golf course and costs only $175,000. You have enough money in your IRA to pay cash for the property, and you intend to do so. But first, you have to decide what would be a decent return on the property. The stock market has not been good to you over the last few years, and at first, you think that you just want to charge enough rent to break even. Then you realize that you're talking about your retirement funds, and that you must increase the value of your IRA on every transaction you make. Although you love your stepson, you know that doing him a favor today will cost you tomorrow.

Your real estate broker informs you that the market rent for a house like this is about $2,000 per month. Through your own calculations, you determine that this will give you a 13-percent return. Well, maybe you can give your stepson a *little* break. You decide that you can live with a 10-percent return, and therefore offer to rent the house to your stepson for $1,500 per month. He gladly accepts. You justify the slightly-below-market rent with the tenant's qualifications—his dependability and the fact that he will assist in the upkeep of the house.

Your real estate broker draws up the purchase agreement for your IRA. Although you are tempted to make only a verbal agreement with your stepson, your good sense tells you that this is a bad idea, so you have your attorney draw up a lease. This, you know, will help prevent problems in the future. Soon, your stepson is making payments to your IRA of $1,500 a month.

Time goes by, and you decide to move south and start playing some golf. You give your stepson a call and tell him that it's time to move on. Because you have generously kept the rent low, he has been able to save enough money to buy a home of his own. You are now over 59½ and retired. You contact your IRA administrator, and tell him that you want to take a disbursement of the golf course home. Because so much time has passed since the home's purchase, the administrator requires an appraisal of the property. You get one and find that in addition to the $1,500 a month you've been receiving over the last few years, the value of your house has appreciated another $75,000. The house is now worth $250,000. That's the good news. The bad news is that if you have a traditional IRA, you will have to pay taxes on the $250,000. If you are in a Roth, though, you are home free. (For more information about making disbursements, see Chapter 11.)

BUYING OPTIONS ON RELATIVES' PROPERTY

If you read Chapter 6, you understand how the option—the written right to purchase property under specific conditions—can help build IRA wealth. But perhaps you didn't realize that you can buy options on property owned by relatives—as long as the family members involved are not among those disqualified from making transactions with your IRA. The following scenario will show you how this type of investment can be arranged, and how it can grow IRAs.

Buying Options With Relatives—A Scenario

Let's say you own a farm or several parcels of land, which you've always planned on passing on to your children when you die. But instead, you are now inspired to gift the land to your kids during your lifetime using your $10,000 per year gift exclusion, which allows each of them to receive annual gifts of $10,000 or less without paying taxes. Bill gets the north forty acres, and Jane gets the east forty acres. It really doesn't matter because each parcel looks just like the next. The parcels are worth a thousand dollars per acre as farm ground now, and someday will be developed into subdivision lots worth tens of thousands.

Four years later, each of your children owns a 40-acre parcel. Together, they own eighty acres of contiguous, path of progress ground. It's not worth a lot today, but it will be someday.

Now comes the fun part. Bill takes an option to purchase Jane's forty acres with his IRA. (Remember, brothers and sisters can deal directly with one another's IRAs.) The IRA's option is for fair market value today ($40,000). It will pay an option price of $1,000 per year to maintain that option for the next ten years. Now, Jane does the same for Bill. Seven or eight years go by. The property has increased tenfold and is now worth $400,000 per parcel, or $800,000 altogether.

A developer comes to the table wanting to buy the property for development into single-family houses. If he buys the property from the children, the $400,000 that each child will receive will be regarded as capital gains. What to do? Instead of selling the land to the developer, Bill and Jane sell their IRA-owned options to the developer. He buys the options for $360,000 each, and the money goes directly into the kids' IRAs. If Bill and Jane used Roth IRAs, the gain is tax-free. If they used traditional IRAs, the gain is tax-deferred. The developer now owns the options and pays each of the children $40,000 for their parcel of land. The only gain reportable is the $40,000.

I've seen this scenario in action with several clients, and it works beautifully. Instead of making their kids wait for land that they'll eventually receive anyway, parents give their children a wonderful gift that they can use right now to prepare for their retirement. Moreover, parents are often able to see their kids benefit from the gift during their lifetimes. As you may have guessed, though, you and your siblings don't have to receive land as a gift to invest in options. You can grow your IRA by buying options on anyone's property, gifted or not, as long as the property's owner is not a disqualified person.

BUYING PROPERTY WITH RELATIVES

Believe it or not, you and your relatives can get together and use your separate IRAs, and discretionary funds as well, to purchase property. This may be done using any one of three different types of ownership, including tenancy-in-common, a limited partnership, and a limited liability company.

In *tenancy-in-common* ownership, which was first discussed in Chapter 4, each of two or more people has an undivided interest in the property, without the right of survivorship. (In other words, upon each partner's death, his share will go to the person designated in his will—not to the other partners.) Further, each party can sell his share without the consent or agreement of the other party. Thus, there is no inherent risk incurred when investing with family members' IRAs in tenancy-in-common relationships. Your IRA owns a piece of the rock, and you can do with it what you will.

A *limited liability company (LLC)*—also first discussed in Chapter 4—is a combination of a corporation and a partnership in which each party buys shares in the property according to what he can invest. The term "limited liability" refers to the fact that like a corporation, the LLC limits personal liability to each of the parties involved, so that members cannot lose more money than they contributed. In other words, their other assets can never be touched. However, an LLC is taxed not like a corporation, but like a partnership in that earnings are taxed only once.

A *limited partnership* is a form of ownership in which there are two types of partners. Limited partners provide financial backing, but have little role in the management of the property and no personal liability for its debts. But general partners, who are responsible for managing the property, have unlimited personal liability. In other words, if someone is a general partner in two or more limited partnerships, and one partnership fails and creates a liability, the general partner's creditors can attach all of his interests in all of his limited partnerships. Both LLCs and limited partnerships differ from tenancy-in-common ownership in that they may or may not enable you to buy or sell at will.

What tenancy-in-common ownership, limited liability companies, and limited partnerships all have in common is that they allow you and other people—including *disqualified persons*—to join forces and make profitable investments. Why? Because when you buy interests in any of these arrangements, you are dealing with the company or the seller—not with the other members. However, while these partnerships are created all the time, doing so safely and correctly requires the assistance of an attorney. In order for the government to permit your IRA to be included in such arrangements, you must address specific legal issues and add specific clauses to the documents involved. In addition, in the case of an LLC or limited partnership, if your group of investors includes disqualified individuals, you must make sure to avoid certain situations that could lead to a prohibited transaction. (Note that this same risk is not posed by tenancy-in-common ownership.) Your attorney is the best person to handle this.

Now that you understand some of the risks involved, we can move on to explore the exciting possibilities! The following scenarios show how different types of family ownership can enable you to invest your IRA funds both safely and profitably.

Buying Property Through an LLC or Limited Partnership—A Scenario

As already mentioned, without violating those rules that govern IRA transactions, you and your relatives can use an LLC to join resources and buy property. Just as important, you—who are also a disqualified person in the eyes of the IRS—can also join resources with your IRA to purchase property. Let's see how it's done.

Let's say that your financial planner tells you about an interesting investment that he feels would provide needed diversity to your investment strategy. A piece of property is being developed into a small neighborhood retail shopping center, with an overall value of about $3 million. The developer of the center has been in business for fifteen years and has a very successful track record. He has already acquired the parcel of ground, completed due diligence, and decided to go forward with the development. Now, he is looking for equity investors—individuals who will purchase equity in the property. This is different from loaning money, as an equity investor is an actual owner who will profit from property appreciation as well as any income generated.

Developers have only two basic ways of raising the money needed to develop and build a project. Either they can borrow the money, or they can take on partners in the project by selling each a piece of the action. If the developer is well heeled, he may choose not to take on any equity investors, and instead use his own resources to complete the project with the help of a friendly bank. Such is not usually the case, though.

In this scenario, the developer needs equity in his project to justify obtaining a loan from his bank. In addition to requiring equity investors, the bank wants to see cash available in case a shortfall or an unexpected glitch in the project occurs. The bank wants to know that the development will definitely be completed. This is where you and your IRA come in.

The developer has more than $1.2 million equity in the project, and is attempting to raise an additional $400,000 to complete the deal. You obtain his prospectus, pass it on to your accountant for review, and get your accountant's blessing. The accountant likes what he sees—especially the fact that the cash-on-cash return to investors will be in the 13-percent range. Better still is the anticipated overall return, which is almost 25 percent annually. (To learn about cash-on-cash and overall returns, see the inset on page 180 of Chapter 9.)

In any case, the minimum share buy-in is $100,000, and you have only $50,000 of savings available in the bank. What to do? You should know the answer to this by now. You turn to your IRA and commit $50,000 from your retirement fund as well as $50,000 from your savings. You then ask the developer to issue a membership interest in each separate name: a half share to you and a half share to your IRA.

"But what about doing business with your IRA?" you ask. "Isn't that taboo?" Well you are not doing business with your IRA. Remember, I said that all three parts of a prohibited transaction must be in place to create a violation. Your IRA plan must be involved, which it is. There must be a disqualified person, which there is—you. And there must be a prohibited transaction between the plan and the disqualified person—which there isn't. You see, the transaction is between the LLC and the plan, and the LLC and the disqualified person—not between the plan and the disqualified person.

Now, let's get your family involved in this investment. Let's say that while your accountant was crunching the numbers, word leaked out that you were on to a good thing, and your brother decided to buy a share of the LLC with his IRA. Again, we don't meet the requirements of a prohibited transaction because we don't have a prohibited transaction between the plan and a disqualified person. In this case, we don't even have a disqualified person. You, your IRA, and your brother's IRA are all doing business *separately* with the LLC.

Could this same investment have been made by forming a limited partnership instead of an LLC? Absolutely! In that case, the developer would have been the general partner, and you and your brother would have been limited partners. What would have been the difference? For you and your brother, there would have been virtually no difference. However, the same could not be said for the developer, who would have had unlimited personal liability for his debts. That's why the LLC is now the legal entity of choice for so many developers.

Buying Property Through Tenancy-in-Common Ownership—A Scenario

If the idea of joining forces with your family appeals to you, you may not want to wait until a great opportunity presents itself. Instead, it may be wiser to bring interested family members together and search for investment properties that will suit the group's needs.

Let's say that you arrange a meeting of prospective investors. Comprised of older family members—including some disqualified persons—the group is approaching retirement and wants a solid, no-hassle investment that returns cash to its investors on a monthly basis. The family can raise $500,000, part with discretionary funds and the rest with IRAs.

145

You call your real estate broker and describe what you're looking for, explaining that you want the investment to provide a minimum annual return of 12 percent on the $500,000 invested. You emphasize the fact that you are not looking for a high leveraged (large mortgage) property. Your primary goals are cash returns and security. The broker is given no limitations other than these. The world is his oyster!

Because your broker is most familiar with his local market, he looks there first. Nothing of any significance is found, though, so he broadens the search and is able to find three properties that fit the bill.

After reviewing all three properties with your group, you decide to pursue a 10,000-square-foot retail/office building in a small town in upstate New York. It is a well-located building in a town of about 12,000 people. The broker's due diligence reveals that it is a stable area of slow growth. He advises you that buildings in small towns do not appreciate at the rate they do in urban areas, because small towns do not provide the high turnover in property sales needed to drive prices upwards rapidly. The flip side, though, is that you will pay less for this small-town property than you would if it were located in a city, and will enjoy an identical cash flow.

You tell your broker to bind the property with a purchase agreement (contract) subject to verifying all of the due diligence he has collected. You make your offer. You then call your accountant and turn the package over to him for verification of the numbers.

Your group decides to take title as tenants-in-common. This arrangement was chosen because it will allow each of you to invest the amount of money he has available, rather than a prescribed share; and because it will allow the participation of disqualified individuals without risking a prohibited transaction. There will be no debt, the tenants will pay all the expenses, and the tenants have several years left on their leases. You hire a local real estate company to keep an eye on the building and collect and disburse the rents to the owners. The attorney draws title as tenants-in-common, completes the IRA administrator's paperwork, and sends it on to the title insurance company. Then the money is sent to the seller, and title passes to the individual "tenants" based on the percentage of ownership purchased by each one. Your family members' IRAs and those members who used discretionary funds start receiving an annual return of 12 percent. Because of this healthy return, most will probably hold this property for years.

What if your family wants to gain wealth instead of developing a steady cash flow? Simply tell your real estate broker what you're looking for, and he'll find the investment that does what you want it to do. If necessary, you may have to split your family into different groups, each of which looks for a property that would help them meet their goal.

BUILDING YOUR CHILD'S IRA

You now know many ways in which you can make your own IRA grow. But how about helping your children establish their IRAs? Is there anything you can do to jump-start their retirement accounts? You know the value of a good retirement nest egg, but kids just don't think of these things. They feel they're invincible. That's why you want to get them started as soon as possible. How? Well, this can be accomplished in at least a couple of ways.

In an earlier scenario, you learned that you can gift land to your children in $10,000-a-year increments. Your kids can then use their IRAs to buy options on one another's property, and eventually reap the benefits of appreciation. This is one way in which you can make their IRAs grow.

What if you don't have any land to gift to your children? Fortunately, there's another way you can give your kids a head start with their retirement funds. In Chapter 1, you learned that you can contribute only earned income or alimony to an IRA. So your three-month-old can't start an IRA, right? Wrong. A three-month-old child can, in fact, have earned income. Let's say that you own a business, and as part of that business, you launch an advertising campaign. Let's further assume that you include your child in your advertisements. It would be only fair to pay her for her work, right? And that money can be claimed as earned income.

All your child needs is a Social Security number. Then put her to work, open an IRA in her name, and start watching it grow.

Perhaps most important, tell your children about the value of preparing for retirement by making wise investments through a self-directed IRA. As they mature and are able to understand some of the basics of investing, explain what you're doing to grow your own IRA wealth. Your flourishing retirement account may be the best means of teaching your kids the value of smart investing and spurring them on to build their own nest eggs.

THE EDUCATION IRA

If you're interested in helping your family through IRA investments—and especially if you're concerned about the future of your children—you'll definitely want to hear about the Education IRA, now called the Coverdell Education Savings Account. The purpose of this IRA is to provide friends and family with a means of paying for a child's education.

This is the way the Education IRA works. Every year, family and friends make contributions, which cannot total more than $2,000 annually, and cannot continue after the beneficiary reaches eighteen years of age. Like contributions to a Roth IRA, these are not deductible. But as long as the gain is used for qualified educational expenses and the beneficiary is under thirty years of age, the withdrawals are tax-free. If money remains in the account when the beneficiary reaches age thirty or has finished his or her education, the funds can be rolled over into an Education IRA for a family member of the original beneficiary. And the legacy goes on.

This IRA is an exceptionally flexible investment tool. Virtually anyone—parents, grandparents, friends, neighbors, and even the child himself—can contribute to an Education IRA. Unlike contributions made to traditional and Roth IRAs, these need not be from earned income. Although many think of the Education IRA as a means of funding college, the money can be used to pay for any qualified educational expenses, whether they are in elementary schools, secondary schools, or college. This means that you can even foot the bill for that expensive prep school across town. The beneficiary can be changed at will to a variety of people, including the original beneficiary's spouse, child, grandchild, stepchild, brother, sister, stepbrother, or stepsister. Moreover, anyone who contributes to an Education IRA can still make contributions to his own IRA. Yes, you read that correctly. You can make your annual contribution of $3,000 to your IRA and contribute up to $2,000 to an Education IRA.

You may be wondering if just like any other Individual Retirement Account, the Education IRA can be built through real estate investments. The scenario below will show you how it works.

Building an Education IRA—A Scenario

Your first grandchild is born, and you and her other grandparents set up an Education IRA, with each of you contributing $500. Because $2,000 is a relatively small amount, you are not able to get much of a return—say, 6 percent. But all of you continue to contribute, and the IRA grows. By the time your grandchild starts school, the IRA holds $12,000 worth of contributions and $2,788 in interest, for a total value of $14,788.

Now the fund is large enough to command better investment returns. For the next six years, the IRA returns 10 percent per year while your contributions continue. When your grandchild is in seventh grade, the IRA is worth $43,172, and you and the other grandparents have each contributed only $500 annually over an eleven-year period. Now you can *really* do something with the IRA.

You put $40,000 of the IRA into a 12-percent note for the next six years, and continue to contribute the annual amount of $2,000 per year, with the new contributions returning only 10 percent. When your grandchild graduates from high school, the IRA is worth a whopping $100,004!

If there is still money left in the account when your grandchild has finished her education, you can name a new beneficiary. If one of the grandparents passes away, you can replace his or her contribution with someone else's. And if you are concerned that the child may not handle the IRA investments correctly, you have the option of directing the IRA yourself. By all means, as the child withdraws money, continue to invest any funds remaining in the account wisely—in real estate, in other words. You may have just built the first educational legacy in your family.

If you are involved in service groups and are always trying to raise money to assist youths, the Education IRA may be just the investment tool you're looking for. What a wonderful gift you would give your community if you set up a few of these for the area's underprivileged children! Just remember to build Education IRA wealth by investing the funds in solid real estate and real estate paper.

AVOIDING THE PITFALLS

So far, this chapter has discussed all the wonderful things that can arise from IRA investments made with family members. In fact, these collaborations are created all the time, and the families who are involved truly reap great benefits. But it would be misleading to imply that such partnerships don't have their pitfalls.

When dealing with family, emotions and misunderstandings can take a perfectly good business deal and turn it bad. Of course, this can happen in any transaction. But when working with your stockbroker or an independent real estate broker, you have a non-personal relationship. If something goes wrong with the investment, it is strictly business. If worst comes to worst, you and your stockbroker or real estate agent can simply part ways. The same cannot be said of investments that include family members. You can't just part ways with your brother or your cousin. That's why I suggest that you document everything, just as you would if you were making a transaction with a stranger. Make your agreements—all of which should be in writing—clear and indisputable. Dot the I's and cross the T's. Let the written word—not you—be the governor of your transactions with the family. More than once, I have seen misunderstandings upset the apple cart of a family deal. From the very start, outline in detail just how your investment relationship is going to work, and who will do what. Make sure that everyone understands the possible risks, and not just the anticipated benefits.

Emotions will always be part of any family undertaking. But if you carefully lay the groundwork for each investment, and if the proper documents are drawn up—documents that clearly reflect the decisions made by you and your relatives—chances are that your IRA investment will run smoothly, yielding considerable returns for you and your loved ones.

Throughout Part Two, you have learned about a range of relatively low-risk investments. These investments may be perfectly suited to both your retirement goals and your tolerance for risk. If so, you can stop right here and use the tools you have just acquired to build your IRA.

But if you're like many investors, you're interested in higher income streams—and you're willing to take the risks necessary to make those streams flow in your direction. If so, Part Three will help you build greater IRA wealth.

PART THREE

High-Return Investments

In Part Two, you learned about the many low-risk investments you can make with your IRA. But perhaps you're a more aggressive investor—someone who knows that to realize bigger gains, you have to take bigger risks. If so, the following three chapters are for you.

In Chapter 5, you learned about buying paper that is in the "senior" payback position. Chapter 8 will teach you all about paper that is not in the prime position. These second- and third-position investments are higher in risk than those discussed in Chapter 5, but, if properly selected, can provide far higher rewards and income streams. Chapter 8 will also show you how to buy property in high-risk situations.

Chapter 9 fills you in on what I regard as speculative investing at its best—investments made with limited liability companies (LLCs). These investments have never been more exciting, and once you understand the concept, it will just be a matter of selecting your product and watching your IRA grow. Moreover, because the LLC allows you to join your money with that of other investors, you can make high-return investments even with relatively little capital. Although this chapter focuses on LLCs, be aware that any of the speculative investments discussed within its pages can also be made with limited partnerships. I have used the LLC in my examples because for many people, it is now the partnership of choice simply because it limits the personal liability of each of the parties involved.

Chapter 10 discusses acquiring ownership of a business with your IRA. If you want to buy the company you work for—or any other business, for that matter—this is where you'll find out how to do it. As you'll learn, there are several ways in which your purchase can be structured so that it is perfectly legal. There are also several ways in which you can make your investment relatively secure—one of which is to buy an enterprise that includes valuable property. This is not to say that such investments don't involve risk. They do. But when thoroughly researched and handled by an able crew, the purchase of a business can provide a nearly limitless stream of income, dramatically adding to IRA wealth.

If you find the investments discussed in Part Three intriguing, but you'd appreciate less risk, you'll find that the following chapters guide you in moderating risk for nearly every investment discussed. Chapter 8, for instance, shows you how to safely loan money to borrowers who don't meet your qualifications in the credit department. You'll learn what to look for in documentation, and you'll discover how to research high-return investments so that you can reduce the hazards. Just remember that although you can minimize risk, you cannot eliminate it.

One last caution is in order before you turn the page. When making these higher-risk investments, it is critical to get help and advice from people who know what they're doing and can guide you, without error, through each investment. While an expert crew is important when making any transaction, it is absolutely essential when sailing the waters of high-risk investments. Rather than leaving you foundering, good crew members will know how to bring you to your destination of a secure retirement. Happy navigating!

8

Buying Higher-Risk Income Streams

*The world turns aside to let any man pass
who knows whither he is going.*

—DAVID STARR JORDAN (1851–1931)

In Chapter 5, you learned how to build IRA wealth through the purchase of real estate-backed notes. In Chapter 4, you discovered how to profit from the purchase of property. While the gains discussed in those chapters were good, even greater income can be obtained by investing in notes and property that involve greater risk. This chapter looks at each of these investments, with a focus on building retirement wealth. Yes, these transactions are not quite as secure as those discussed earlier in the book. But, as you'll learn, there are many ways you can reduce risk. In fact, this chapter concludes with a special section that guides you in performing the research necessary to keep your retirement fund secure. Moreover, each scenario suggests strategies that can turn high-risk situations into IRA wealth-building investments.

BUYING HIGH-RISK NOTES

You can reap huge rewards by using your IRA to buy notes— gains dreamed of only in the stock market. However, to do so, you have to accept more risk. You've already learned about notes that are in senior position, meaning that there are no liens before them. In this chapter, I'd like to make you aware of notes that are in an inferior lien position to these firsts. Called *seconds, thirds, fourths,* etc., according to their payback position, these notes are higher in risk because the proceeds from the sale of the assets securing the note will go to the owner of a superior or senior note before they go to that of a junior note.

How much greater is the reward for junior loans? Quite a bit, actually. While you might receive a return of 12 percent on a well-secured first note, a second may command 14 to 16 percent, and a third or fourth, even more. It is vital, though, to structure the notes correctly, minimizing risk while creating a high income stream. Let's look at a few ways in which this can be done. (For detailed information on investing in notes backed by real estate, see Chapter 5.)

Buying a Note—A Scenario

Five years ago, Joe and Sue bought a rental house. The price of the house was $100,000, and they used $20,000 of their savings and an $80,000 loan from the bank to make the purchase. This $80,000 loan is in senior position. The bank used a good title company to make sure of that before closing the loan. This means that if Joe and Sue forfeit the home to the bank, the bank will be able to get clear title to the house without paying other bills.

The roof of the rental house has developed problems, and has to be replaced. Joe and Sue don't have the $5,000 needed to fix it, but it's not something they can put off. They decide to borrow more money on the house. They know that they could probably refinance the first note, making it larger, and use the extra cash to pay for the roof. But they decide against this option because the first loan is at a favorable interest rate, and the current rate is 3 percent higher. Another option is to take a second independent loan against the property. The second loan would be made at a higher rate of interest, too, but the rate would apply only to the $5,000—not to the whole $85,000. With the second loan in place, the couple would have to pay an additional $100 a month—$700 instead of $600.

While Joe and Sue have been trying to solve their financial problem, you have been searching for good IRA investments. Wisely, you let people know that you're interested in funding loans. As a result, a mutual friend tells you about Joe and Sue's dilemma, and you offer to loan them the money from your IRA.

As a savvy investor, you are aware of the risk you will assume by making this loan. There is an $80,000 loan in front of yours, so if Joe and Sue default on their loan to the bank and the bank takes the property back, you will get the money owed you only if the sale of the house, and the resulting payment of debt to the bank, leaves sufficient money to also cover your note. Understanding the importance of due diligence in all investments—but especially in high-risk investments—you have your broker investigate the property, and discover that it has appreciated by $20,000 in the five years that Joe and Sue have owned it. This means that they will have $35,000 worth of equity in the house after you loan them the $5,000. (To reach this figure, you subtract the bank loan and your loan from the $100,000 purchase price. You then add the resulting figure—$15,000—to the $20,000 of appreciation, for a total of $35,000.)

Encouraged by the increased worth of the property, you tell your attorney to draft the note. In it, he includes a clause stating that "failure to pay on the first was a default on the second." This means that even if your note and the bank's note are both in default, you can forestall foreclosure by the bank and start your own foreclosure. If this actually took place, one of two things would occur. You could foreclose and own a house with $80,000 owed against it. Or you could be required by the first lien holder (the bank) to pay off the note to them. Yes, you would have to satisfy the bank's loan in some way—by refinancing, by bringing the loan payments current, or by renegotiating—but once that was done, there would be $35,000 worth of equity waiting for you.

What would be your return if Joe and Sue did not default on their loan, but were able to make their monthly payments on both notes? Because this note is riskier than one in first position, let's assume that it provides 14-percent interest. Remember: With risk comes reward. Let's further assume that the term of the loan is three years, which includes monthly interest-only payments of $58.33, and a final balloon payment of the principal. If collected as agreed, the $5,000 IRA money you invested would grow to $7,100 in the three-year period of the loan.

You now know why a note in second position involves greater risk than one in first position. Understandably, if you go into third or fourth position, you will take on even greater risk because you will then have not one, but two or three loans to satisfy if the note goes sour.

Other Ways to Lower Your Risk When Buying Notes

In the above scenario, you saw how you can secure high returns and minimize risk by performing good due diligence, and structuring the note in a way that protects your investment. But this isn't the only way you can achieve greater security when buying higher-risk notes.

If the borrower has less-than-perfect credit, you can lower your risk by asking him to add more collateral in the form of additional real estate. Let's say that you are loaning $10,000 on a $20,000 lot. On the surface, it looks like a good investment, but the borrower's credit is suspect. However, your research reveals that he owns a rental house as well. Worth $80,000, this second property has a first mortgage of $40,000. By adding the rental house to the security, you will be in first position on the lot and second position on the rental house. This will tie up more of the borrower's equity, which will not only give him more reason to be timely in his payments, but will also provide a larger return should you have to foreclose.

Another simple way to lower your risk is to add signature strength. Let's say that your real estate broker brings you an opportunity to loan $30,000 at 14-percent interest on a lot in Rigins, Idaho. You have verification that the lot is worth $70,000, so this is probably a decent deal. The problem is that the borrower had less than sterling credit. While there is plenty of equity behind the loan, the last thing you want to own is a lot in Rigins, Idaho. So you ask the borrower to provide additional signature strength. As it turns out, his father has excellent credit and is willing to guarantee the loan. Therefore, you have both the borrower and his father sign the note. Now, both the property and dad's wallet are behind the loan. This has not only made your investment more secure, but has also helped the borrower establish better credit.

A third way to lower your risk is to restructure the ownership of the property. Let's say that the owner of an office building in Nantucket, Massachusetts is in need of a loan on his building. You live in Tyler, Texas. The building checks out as being sound, but the borrower's credit is weak. It is decided that the borrower will sell a portion to a creditworthy borrower, and they will own it together as tenants-in-common. (See page 142 of Chapter 7 to learn about tenancy-in-common ownership.) Both of the borrowers then sign the loan, giving your IRA a better-secured note.

A fourth way to make a high-risk loan more secure is to pay off some of the debt that's in a superior position to yours. Let's say that you have an opportunity to make a 20-percent return. The borrower has a small apartment building in Gainesville, Florida, and needs $50,000 to put on a new roof and make other repairs. Due diligence shows the property value to be $400,000 if the repairs are completed. The borrower has only fair credit, though, and worse than that, there are already three notes on the property, totalling $155,000. It seems that every time the owner repairs the property, he borrows a little more against it. What should you do? You can reduce the risk by reducing the debt. In other words, you can loan the borrower an additional $50,000, for a total of $100,000. In this case, the larger loan allows the borrower to pay off the second and third notes, putting you in second position instead of fourth. You can further cut your risk by putting $50,000 of the loan in an escrow account, to be released as the renovation progresses. That way, you will be assured that the work is completed, and that the property will truly be worth $400,000. You set your interest rate at 18 percent, which means that you will be receiving $1,500 per month during the term of the loan. If the borrower defaults, you will still have to satisfy the first note, but that's a lot less complicated than satisfying three.

BUYING HIGH-RISK PROPERTY

Problems sometimes arise when loaning money on out-of-state property—especially when foreclosure seems probable. You see, foreclosure laws differ from state to state, and it is a must to know these laws before you enter into any high-risk loan. You can, of course, educate yourself about the laws of the state involved in every possible transaction. But this will take time and money, and may drive you a little crazy as you research investment properties in different areas.

Earlier in the chapter, you learned various ways of structuring a loan so that you can help avoid foreclosing on the property. Another option is to buy the property rather than loaning money on it. The following scenarios will show how this can work to the advantage of your retirement account. (For detailed information on buying real estate, see Chapter 4.)

Buying High-Risk Property—Scenario 1

Your real estate broker tells you of an opportunity in Montana. A developer in Boseman has finished one phase of a two-phase sub-division. The first phase of twenty lots has almost been sold out, and it is time to get the second phase of thirty lots ready for marketing. In the second phase, the roads, which were roughed in, need finishing; power has to be brought in; and a water system has to be developed. The developer requires $90,000 to get the additional thirty lots up and running.

The lots in Phase I sold for $25,000 each. Several homes have already been built on the lots, and others are getting started. Your broker is convinced that this is an opportunity to make some money. After your accountant reviews and analyzes the figures from Phase I and the projections for Phase II, you, too, decide that this is a promising investment. The problem is that you live in Canton, Ohio, and know absolutely nothing about Montana law. What if the developer goes under? How will you go about foreclosing? How long would it take? What will it cost? Your intuition tells you that you don't want to make the loan. Yet, you believe in the project.

Rather than loaning money to the developer, you decide to purchase the property. You will give him $90,000 for the thirty lots. While they will be worth $25,000 apiece when the infrastructure goes in, they are probably worth only about $10,000 apiece now. With $300,000 of security for your $90,000 investment, you have eliminated a lot of the risk.

You offer the developer a first option on the property. (To learn about options, see page 107.) The option will allow him to buy back the property for $103,500 total. To keep the option current, he must pay a monthly option price of $1,125 per month, which will apply to the purchase price. He has the option for twelve months. You will now receive 15-percent interest on your investment. Had you structured a straight loan instead of the sale option, the financial result would have been identical. You would have received $1,125 per month, just as you will now. The difference is that should the developer miss an option payment, the option will be over, and you will have the right to resell a property that is worth $300,000 or more—after making an investment of only $90,000. You won't have to foreclose, which can take from five to six months. You will be able to immediately resell the property to someone else.

Buying High-Risk Property—Scenario 2

Your broker approaches you again. He has found a good property for sale—good, but vacant. The office building, located in San Diego, California, is in a nice section of town, but the rental vacancies are a little high at this time. This is one of those phenomena that occur in real estate. When there is a need for a certain product—office buildings, in this case—the builders go crazy constructing offices until there is a glut on the market. With time, the demand again catches up to the supply—and then off the builders go again.

Assuming that you've found a good building in a good area, the best time to buy is when the market is overbuilt. The prices will reflect the glut, and you will get a great buy. What good does it do to purchase a vacant building? It's true that it brings in no income. But your job is to change that.

The owner holds the building free and clear of debt. He has found another investment opportunity, and needs the equity out of this building to use on the next transaction. He would go to the bank and borrow the money, but alas, the bank doesn't want to make a loan on a vacant building. The owner's only choice is to sell. But, considering the soft market, who will pay a decent price?

You offer to purchase the property with your IRA for the asking price of $300,000, subject to the owner's leasing the property back for a period of time. How long? However long you think it will take for the market to firm up. The seller now has to pay you $2,500 in lease payments per month. More important, he has just freed up $300,000 in cash for his next investment. If you are concerned about his credit, you can have him pay the lease up-front—say, one year's worth, or $30,000.

You give the seller the option of subleasing the property. This will secure your investment further, since when the seller sublets the property, you will end up with not just his signature on the lease, but also that of the subtenant. You now not only have your real estate broker looking for a tenant for the building, but you have a very motivated lessee looking, as well. The sooner the seller/lessee gets you a tenant, the sooner he will be off the hook. Nothing will take your risk completely away, but this will greatly limit it.

What if the property were laden with $200,000 debt? Would the seller be willing to complete the same transaction? If he needed the $100,000 equity in cash, he would. If the current $200,000 was payable to the bank at 8-percent interest over twenty years, his payments would be $1,673 per month. For another $827 per month ($2,500 lease less $1,673 = $827), he would solve his problem. Not only would he have the cash he needs, but he would reduce a long-term liability ($1,673 per month for twenty years) to a short-term liability ($2,500 per month only until he sublets the building).

Buying High-Risk Property—Scenario 3

This time, your broker has found three possible properties for you. All look good, but bring with them a certain degree of risk.

The first investment is an interior lot in a commercial subdivision. If the county goes forward with its plans, the lot will end up having highway frontage, which will boost the property's value from its current price of $45,000 to around $100,000. The broker's due diligence has shown that the road will be constructed in three years at best—*if* the highway is approved. The problem is that it's too early to tell for sure if the highway will be completed.

The second property is a small proposed subdivision that the developer is trying to get annexed to the city. If this occurs, the property will have city services and will increase in value from $120,000 to $240,000. The developer believes that the annexation will take place at the county's next planning meeting, scheduled six months hence.

The third property is undergoing a zoning change that will turn an agricultural area into one that will allow twelve housing units per acre. The five acres of farmland are currently selling for $10,000 per acre, but will be worth $50,000 an acre if the change takes place. That could take a while, though, because opposition to the change is great.

You have enough money in your IRA to buy all three properties. The problem is that if they all go sour, you will have had $215,000 invested for several years without a return. You may make a couple of bucks on the resale if the projects fail, but not much more than inflation—and you know that that won't get you far. On the other hand, the possible returns are enormous.

You decide to share both the wealth and the risk. After talking with your crew and some family members about the investments, you find that both your father and your attorney want to play. Using tenancy-in-common ownership (see page 142), your IRA buys a third of each of the properties separately; your dad, another third; and your attorney, another third. If all of the investments go sour, you will now have put up only $71,666 instead of the whole $215,000.

As it turns out, two of the three investments perform as hoped. The highway lot does not end up with a highway, but you are able to sell it for $50,000 after holding it for three years. By the time you pay for the closing costs, you break even on the investment. However, the annexation project goes just as planned, and you are able to flip the property for $200,000 only nine months after purchasing it. The third investment takes longer than expected to generate the anticipated return, but after a three-year battle with the county and the community, the proposed zoning change is approved and the property sells for $250,000. Let's look at how well you did:

	INVESTMENT	RETURN	ANNUALIZED YIELD
Highway Property	$15,000	$0	0 percent
Annexed Property	$40,000	$26,667	89 percent
Zoned Property	$16,667	$66,667	133 percent
Totals	$71,667	$93,334	74 percent

The above table shows that you invested a total of $71,667 and received a total return of $93,334, for an annualized average return of 74 percent. Would you have made more money if you had taken all of the investments on yourself? Sure. But, aware of the risks, you opted for a smaller return. If you continue to make investments like these, your IRA will thrive.

MINIMIZING YOUR RISK

When making any investment, whether high- or low-risk, the key to realizing gains is your ability to compile, review, and understand the due diligence on that particular investment. Most of us are neither financial experts nor experts in the field of real estate investment. We can, however, examine an individual project and determine the risks involved with a reasonable amount of certainty. And by performing thorough research and choosing property with good equity and other factors that favor success, we can greatly improve the security of our investment in even the highest-risk transactions.

To begin, never take another person's word on the advisability of investing in a particular project. Make sure that the advice is backed up by hard data—by an appraisal, for instance, or by income and cash flow statements that demonstrate income. That is why you hired your crew. It is the job of both the broker and the attorney to provide documentation that proves the worthiness of each potential investment.

When buying a note in second or third position, make sure you have a title report that states what is in front of you on the title. In addition, when the title report is requested, ask for documents that are an *exception* to the title, meaning that they restrict your usage of the property. The title report typically includes a list of any exceptions, which may include easements, taxes owed, liens, etc. If there is a lien recorded in front of your lien, be sure to review the recorded document. Why? What if that lien contains a clause stating that if any other liens are recorded against the property, they have the right to call their note due? What if the note in front of yours matures two years before your note does? These are all facts that you have to know.

Whenever possible, obtain a credit report on the borrower of the loan. I say "whenever possible" because if you are not originating the loan—if you are buying an existing note—you probably won't have that option. It's only when you originate a loan that you can easily obtain a credit report. Moreover, as an individual, you can't pull a credit report on someone else. You can, however, have that individual pull his or her own report. Anyone can go on the Internet, search for "credit report," and order one for himself whenever he so desires. If the borrower has good credit, great! If he doesn't, ask yourself if there's any way you can restructure the transaction to reduce your risk.

If there is no appraisal available on the property used as security for the loan, have your real estate broker research comparable properties in the area. Make yourself comfortable. Never enter into an investment without knowing all that you can possibly know about the people and the product. Sound like a lot of work? It's not, because the work will be done by your crew members. Use your title company to perform title searches, and your broker to determine market values and rents. Have your attorney review existing leases and other documents. And if you start getting confused by the numbers, call in your accountant. The few hundred dollars you spend on these professionals will be peanuts compared with what you have to risk.

In this chapter, you have learned how to make a variety of investments that are high in risk but also high yielding. If these discussions have piqued your interest in high-return investments, you'll love Chapter 9, which spotlights the ultimate investment vehicle—the limited liability company.

The LLC–Speculative Investing at Its Best

The business of America is business.

—CALVIN COOLIDGE (1872–1933)

One of the most popular real estate investments in recent years has been the Real Estate Investment Trust, or REIT. REITs are professionally managed portfolios of real estate properties. The company combines the money of several investors and uses it to buy, maintain, and sell real estate, hopefully at a profit. Because it pools the money of so many people, the REIT is able to invest in comparatively high-priced properties—a freedom not enjoyed by the individual investor, who generally has more limited means. The problem is that as a stockholder, you are one of many, with no decision-making powers regarding the investments that are being purchased and held by the REIT. Plus, the costs of running a REIT often eat up as much as 35 percent of the profits, diminishing the value of the shares.

What if you could increase your investment power, but still maintain control of each and every investment—*and* enjoy the limited liability offered by stocks? Although it may sound too good to be true, it's not. This chapter explores the limited liability company, or LLC, and shows how you can use it to join forces with experienced developers, and profit from the construction of housing developments and shopping centers. As you'll soon discover, the LLC not only boosts your investment options while allowing you to choose your investments, but provides a number of other benefits as well. That's why I consider the LLC the ultimate investment vehicle for speculative investors who want to increase their retirement funds to the max.

It should be noted at this point that, as first discussed in Chapter 7, all of the investments that can be made through an LLC can also be made through a limited partnership. (See page 142 to learn about the limited partnership.) However, because all members of an LLC have personal liability protection, while the general manager of a limited partnership does not, the LLC is now the partnership of choice for many investors. Thus, in this chapter, I have used the term "limited liability company" to refer to both types of partnerships, either of which can be used to build IRA wealth.

WHAT IS A LIMITED LIABILITY COMPANY?

A *limited liability company* (LLC) is a combination of a corporation and a partnership in which each party buys shares in a property according to what he can invest. Many experts say that the LLC combines the *best* characteristics of corporations and partnerships. How? Well, the LLC is a separate legal entity like a corporation, and therefore offers personal liability protection in that you, as a member, cannot lose more money than you contribute. However, for tax purposes, it is entitled to be treated as a partnership in that earnings are taxed only once. This is different from a standard or C corporation, which, in effect, pays taxes twice. First, the corporation itself pays taxes; then, the stockholders pay taxes on their gains.

WHY FORM A LIMITED LIABILITY COMPANY?

You've already learned some of the advantages of the LLC. For instance, the LLC offers personal liability protection, and its income is taxed only once, which means larger returns for its members. But the LLC offers other benefits, as well. An LLC is comparatively easy to run. Like a sole proprietorship, there is no statutory necessity to keep minutes, hold meetings, or make resolutions. Moreover, the LLC has great flexibility, with each company free to establish an organizational structure agreed upon by its members. Thus, it can be managed by its members, in which case it operates like a partnership, or it can elect a manager. This is important, as in most cases, IRS rules prohibit you from managing any investment funded by your retirement account, making it necessary to elect a manager who is not investing with his IRA.

The LLC offers another special advantage to the IRA investor, as it permits both you and disqualified individuals—your parents and your children, for instance—to take part in the same investment. In such a case, your IRA and each disqualified individual hold a separate membership interest in the LLC. (To learn more about making investments with disqualified individuals, see Chapter 7.) Such an arrangement also allows you to invest both IRA funds and your own discretionary funds in a single venture.

Because of all these advantages, the LLC is a wonderful means of investing in land development. And such investments can bring high yearly returns. In my experience, I have seen LLCs yield annual returns from 15 percent to 118 percent! Of course, these investments are higher in risk than many of those discussed earlier in the book. You wouldn't be getting big returns if they weren't. But with good due diligence, you can lower the risk while maintaining returns realized in few other investments.

YOUR CREW

If you have read earlier chapters in this book, you know that an able crew is important when making any investment, but is absolutely *vital* when making a high-risk investment.

Your real estate broker, for instance, will be invaluable in finding suitable properties in which your IRA can invest. When investing at this level, you must have confidence in your broker's experience. You don't want to use the brother-in-law who just got his real estate license, and you probably don't want to rely on the broker whose experience has been confined to house hunting. You want someone who is aware of all the development investment opportunities around you, and can use an extensive network of connections to find developers and builders in need of financing. Your broker should also have contacts in other geographical areas so that he can anticipate emerging markets. And he should have the ability to perform good due diligence and present you with all the information you need to evaluate each investment property.

Your accountant should understand your goals and know the level of risk with which you are comfortable. He must be able to tell good numbers from bad, and be forthright in his evaluation of each potential investment. If you followed the guidelines provided in Chapter 3 for choosing a professional with real estate experience, your accountant should have the skills you need. Just don't forget to involve him in the assessment of potential investments. His input is important.

When working with an LLC, you need a real estate or employee benefits attorney who understands contract law, real estate law, and IRA regulations. You will want an LLC agreement that protects your principal. And you will want an opt-out clause—a firm date at which the IRA can opt out of the investment. A good attorney will make sure not only that the agreement is legal and in keeping with IRS rules, but also that it will safeguard your IRA wealth.

Of course, your IRA administrator will have its usual job of reviewing the investment, arranging funding, and sending appropriate paperwork to the IRS. Because an LLC agreement can be complex, I recommend running it past your administrator before it's signed. It's much easier to make changes to a new document than it is to add addendums to an old one. Once the agreement has been approved by your administrator and signed by all parties, it can then be sent to the administrator for funding.

At this point, everyone in your crew is ready for action. Now it's time to find an investment that will give you not a good return, but a *great* return.

USING THE LIMITED LIABILITY COMPANY

The limited liability company will enable you to make speculative investments that will greatly increase your IRA wealth. However, as you well know, speculative investments can also be risky. If you are to protect your retirement money, you must make sure that your attorney includes several components in each agreement. Therefore, we are first going to discuss some LLC agreement basics. After that, the real fun will began as you read scenarios— all modeled on real-life investments—that show how these basics can be used to grow IRA wealth.

LLC Agreement Basics

If you've followed the guidelines provided in this book for assembling an able crew, you're now working with an attorney who's well versed in both real estate law and contract law. Nevertheless, if you want to keep your retirement money secure, you won't place blind trust in your lawyer as he drafts the agreements for your limited liability companies. Instead, you'll make certain that several clauses are, when appropriate, made part of your LLC contracts.

First, always keep in mind that you worked hard to build your retirement fund, and should do everything you can to protect your principal. The risk should be taken on the profit side, not on the principal side. A great way to do this is to follow the cash-in-cash-out rule. To understand this, consider an investment in land development. You and a land developer form an LLC together. You invest cash, thereby buying equity in the LLC. (This is called *hard equity*.) The developer, whom you are funding, may have also used some cash to purchase the land, and therefore may have some hard equity. However, he has also "purchased" equity not with cash, but by making improvements to the property. (This is called *soft equity* or *sweat equity*.) The LLC agreement should state that the LLC members who put in cash for their equity should get the first cash resulting from the sale of the investment. Once these members have received their principal back from the investment, the soft equities will be paid proportionately. After that, the profits will be split based on each member's percentage of ownership. This arrangement will increase your chances of getting your principal back even if the investment does not turn out as well as expected. In some cases, I have even structured the contract so that, although the developer had hard equity in the property, he had to wait until all of the investors received their principal back before having his own cash returned. I call this an incentive clause, as it gives the developer a good deal of incentive to complete the project in a timely and efficient manner.

Second, remember that as a member of the LLC, you cannot turn in your shares whenever you have the whim to do so. Therefore, when making any long-term investment with an LLC—one of more than four years' duration—the agreement should include an opt-out clause that provides a firm date at which your IRA or any other investor can pull out of the investment. Let's say that you have invested in a retail development. Let's further assume that it will take a year to build the development and another year to lease all of the spaces in the building, and that the developer will then want a year or two of rent stabilization before going to a lender to refinance the project and pay back costs. If the project is not performing as expected, this—the third or fourth year—is a good point at which to place your opt-out clause and sell your membership shares to the LLC for their current value, so that you can reinvest elsewhere. Of course, if the investment shows great promise and no other deal is in the offing, you may instead choose to stay in the LLC for the long haul.

Be aware that although opt-out clauses are a must in long-term investments, you may want to use them even in three- or four-year deals. Consider critical time frames to determine when an opt-out would be advisable. When does the developer expect the project to be at a break-even point? When will the limited liability company be in the best position to buy your shares? The answers to these questions will help you decide if and when you want this clause added. That's why it's so crucial for you to carefully research and completely understand each project before getting involved.

Finally, the LLC's operating agreement must include a clause which states that its shares are transferable. This will allow you to transfer these assets to another entity if and when you decide to change IRA administrators.

Now you're familiar with the basics of making speculative investments through an LLC. The following scenarios show how these basics can be put to use to build retirement wealth.

Using an LLC—Scenario 1

You have developed a close working relationship with your real estate broker over the years. Now you are only ten or so years from retirement, and you send your broker out to find an investment that will really pay off—one that will enable you to look forward to a retirement that is not just secure, but truly enjoyable.

After a thorough search, your broker finds a possible investment in Omaha, Nebraska. There, a developer is buying large parcels of farmland at farm prices, subdividing them into single-family lots, and reselling the lots to homeowners and home-builders. The developer has used $500,000 of his own money to purchase the land, and is trying to raise another $500,000 to develop the property. When the lots are sold—presumably by the end of year two—he expects to realize a profit of $1 million. He is willing to give up some of that profit in exchange for the needed funding.

This is a pretty standard investment. Your broker provides you with appraisals of the land both "as is" and as a subdivision, and you are satisfied that the value is there. The broker also provides you with the developer's construction costs and time schedule, as well as his marketing plan. Moreover, after investigating the developer's background and previous projects, the broker allays any concerns you might have about the developer's ability to complete the project. You take all of that information to your accountant, and ask him to review it for accuracy and viability. He confirms that the venture is a sound one.

One of the aspects of this project that appeals to both you and your accountant is the profit margin. Because there are so many unknowns in land development, you wisely insist on seeing a 100-percent profit margin going into the development. In other words, the profit must be equal to the combined costs of buying, developing, and marketing the property. True, there are developers who work on a large scale, and have had so much experience on similar projects that they've been able to fine-tune their costs, and therefore need smaller profit margins. But even when replicating past projects, a developer may encounter risks that could never be anticipated. During my years of investment, for instance, I have seen delays caused by flooding due to above-average rainfall; by contaminants found on the property; and by numerous other problems. Aware of all the "hiccups" that can occur during development, you know that a 100-percent markup is not out of line. And this is exactly the profit margin offered by this project. ($1 million for land purchase and development, and $1 million profit.) You decide to go forward with the investment.

It's time to meet with the developer and your attorney to discuss the terms of the LLC agreement. The healthy profit margin has helped reduce your risk, but you want to do even more to protect your retirement money. That's the purpose of the agreement—to minimize your risk, and maximize your profits.

In this very simple example, the developer has put up $500,000 and you have put up $500,000. You might think that the profit would be split the same way: 50-50. However, that's probably not how it will work. As discussed earlier, you, as an investor, may choose to pull out of the investment at some point, but the developer will have to oversee the project and take it to its completion. He therefore has quite a bit more at stake than you. So what type of split is reasonable? For your investment of $500,000, the developer may be willing to sell you 30 to 35 percent of the ownership. That means that if all goes as planned, within a couple of years, you will receive a return of up to $350,000 on your $500,000 investment. Is this really possible? Yes, yes, yes.

You and the developer settle on an ownership split of 35 percent to 65 percent, with your IRA owning the smaller share. You instruct your attorney to prepare an LLC agreement that reflects this split, and that makes the developer the managing member of the LLC. This means that, within certain limits, the developer will be calling the shots on this project. You know that because of the developer's extensive experience, he is best qualified to make decisions about the development. Moreover, you know that in most cases, IRS rules prohibit you from managing an investment made with your retirement account.

To insure that your principal will be returned to your IRA, the agreement states that the developer will get his $500,000 back only after you receive your $500,000. This clause pretty much guarantees that your money will be returned to you. Remember that the original cost of the property was $500,000. Once the land is improved with roads, utilities, etc., it will definitely be worth more. The only question is "How much more?" That's where you're taking a chance. Once the developer gets a return of his principal, the profits will be distributed, with 65 percent going to him and 35 percent going to your IRA. Do you add an opt-out clause to the agreement? Yes. The builder has indicated that it will take him two years to complete the project, so you have asked for a two-year opt-out date. At that point, you can choose to take whatever profits have been generated and move on to another investment. Of course, if the development is going well at that point, but not all the lots have been sold, you may very well decide to remain in the LLC past that date.

The agreement is signed, and the development is completed as planned. Your IRA receives a 70-percent return on your investment, or 35 percent a year. Not bad.

You might remember that earlier, I spoke of "hiccups" that can occur during development. So before we leave this scenario, let's give this investment a couple and see what happens. First, let's say that just as the infrastructure is being constructed, the county places a moratorium on sewer hookups because it has run out of capacity. Because the lots won't sell without sewers, this essentially shuts down the project for eighteen months, at which point further capacity will have been added. The good news is that this property has no debt, so you don't have to deal with that monthly dragon. However, instead of a two-year investment, you end up with a three-and-a-half-year investment. How does this affect your IRA? Well, it still receives a 70-percent return. In this case, though, the return is spread over a longer period of time, making your annual return only 20 percent. This is still a great return.

Now, let's give the project a different problem. Let's say that the developer dies in a hunting accident, and you have to bring another developer onboard. In this case, you may lose a portion of the anticipated return because of additional costs. Instead of making $1 million, you may make only $800,000. It's just as likely, though, that during construction, property prices will move steadily upwards and the development will make $1.2 million in profit! Keep in mind that compared with the risks involved in stock market investments, your risks here, while undeniable, are minimal. Most likely, your principal will be safe because the developer won't make his money back until you do. And I think you'll agree that the potential rewards are well worth the risk.

Before we leave this scenario, a final tip is in order. Once you've invested with a successful developer, follow him to his next project. Why look elsewhere and start anew in your due diligence? Successful developers are likely to continue their success from project to project. Work with them, and they'll help you build IRA wealth.

Using an LLC—Scenario 2

In the first scenario, you enhanced your retirement fund by investing in land development. The developer, partially funded by your IRA, broke a large piece of land into smaller pieces, added basic facilities, and sold the lots on the retail market. As you have seen, this type of investment can be quite profitable. But the following scenario will show that even more profit can be made by seeing a project through from beginning to end—from the purchase of the raw land, to the construction of the buildings, to the sale of the fully improved property.

Let's say that your real estate broker finds an investment that is just getting started in the Lacy, Washington area. He has already met with the developer and has found that over the past decade or so, the man has successfully completed a number of similar developments. Apparently, this developer had a knack for finding and acquiring land packages with one-hundred-percent locations. In real estate lingo, a *one-hundred-percent location* is a site that is far superior to other sites in that area. It may be a corner of an intersection that has an extremely high traffic count, or it may be a site that has a commanding view or unusual access, but it is the best site in that vicinity.

In this particular case, the property is on a major thoroughfare at an intersection that already commands high traffic. It has access from two sides, and a traffic light that stops the many vehicles which pass each day. The developer acquired the land two years ago, and has been preparing it for development ever since. He has changed the zoning to allow for commercial development, and has had his engineers and architects draw lot lines and prepare a conceptual view of a small neighborhood office/retail park. He has also obtained preliminary approval for dividing the property into five individual lots that include a restaurant site, two retail buildings, and two office buildings. This plan is consistent with his earlier projects. An appraisal of the completed project estimates a final value of $5 million.

Already, this project sounds like a winner, but more good news follows. During the two years of planning, the surrounding area has exploded with big national stores and distribution sites, adding to the area's traffic count. Apartment development has grown as well. Originally purchased for a price of $900,000, the developer's site is now valued at more than $1.5 million. He could sell the site, take the profits, and run, but he knows that the real profits come from owning a completed project. Because he has experience, he has set up his limited liability company to accommodate IRAs. The language necessary to qualify for IRA membership was put into the formation of the LLC agreement.

The developer has approached a bank about funding the construction, and has obtained a commitment, subject to his meeting two requirements. The first requirement is that the developer obtain leases for at least 50 percent of the proposed space prior to construction. The second requirement is that the developer have an additional $500,000 equity in the property. The developer has already found tenants for the property in excess of 50 percent. He now has to find additional funding to the tune of $500,000.

You and your broker hear opportunity knocking. If you were to loan $500,000 to the developer, you would receive a nice return—say 12 percent. But because your IRA will share in the risk of the development stage of the project, a higher return will be expected—from 15 to 25 percent, or even more.

The developer provides a prospectus that states his background and details the other players in the project, such as the engineering firm and the project manager, as well as the list of tenants who have signed commitments to lease. You are able to examine the construction costs, the bank's commitment to fund the construction, and the appraisal. Included in the prospectus are a projected cash flow statement, an annual property operating data (APOD) statement, and, of course, the LLC operating agreement. All in all, it's a lot of data for you to review. While doing so, you keep in mind that projected numbers are just that—educated guesses based on market studies and past performance. These figures may be conservative or may be pie-in-the-sky numbers. To make sure that you can tell one from the other, you bring in your accountant, who can confirm the numbers for you. You also bring in your attorney, who must review the leases and the LLC agreement.

When you and your accountant review the prospectus, you find that of the 13,400 square feet available in this project, the developer has obtained leases on 7,300 square feet (54.48 percent of the total), so you know that he has met the requirements for the bank loan. According to the developer's cash flow analysis, the cash-on-cash return will start at 10.25 percent the second year, and will increase by about 1 percent each year. The overall return—which takes into consideration equity buildup due to mortgage paydown and appreciation—projects an even healthier return. (See the inset on page 180 to learn about cash-on-cash and overall returns.) The anticipated overall return is 25.1 percent for the second year, with a 2-percent increase expected every year thereafter. At the end of the fourth year, the property is expected to show a cash flow of over 14 percent and an overall return of almost 29 percent. Is this unusual? Absolutely not. These are the kinds of returns you should expect. You may ask yourself why you would make this kind of investment when the previous scenario provided a 35-percent return for investing in land alone. Well, in the type of investment discussed in Scenario 1, when the land runs out, the returns run out, too. In this case, though, the returns are like the Energizer Bunny. They just keep going and going.

Your accountant double-checks the numbers and believes them to be realistic. Your attorney reviews the leases and the LLC operating agreement, and also seems satisfied. You decide to invest $200,000 in the LLC. You add a clause regarding the cash-in-cash-out rule, which will come into play only upon the sale of the property. At that point, the profit will go first to those who invested cash, and will then be distributed among the other members of the LLC. The distributions that will be made in the years before the sale will reduce the cash-in-cash-out issue, but will probably not return the investment by the time of the sale.

Life goes on, and the buildings are built and leased. After about three and a half years, you take a hard look at your investment and notice that the returns are not quite what you thought they would be. Your overall cash flow has averaged only 10 percent per year, and your overall return has been only 20 percent. Why? Well, there were some cost overruns in construction, and it took a little longer than anticipated to get the buildings leased. The return hasn't been bad, but you are a picky investor and know of another investment that could do much better. Fortunately, your agreement includes an opt-out clause, so you let the developer know that you're going to use it.

The developer has anticipated your decision. After all, he agreed to the timing of the opt-out clause when the agreement was signed. The buildings have been up and running for a couple of years now, and the rents and expenses have stabilized to the point where the development looks good to the bank. Therefore, the bank is willing to provide additional financing based on the new income stream provided by the tenants. It has even offered a lower interest rate, making it possible for the developer to obtain the cash needed to buy back your shares.

Before taking out the loan, though, the developer offers your shares to other LLC members, who bought in after you did. Unlike you, they are quite happy with a 20-percent return, and they decide to buy up your shares. The developer may still go after the new loan just because of its reduced rate, but with or without it, he will be able to pay you off. You will get your money back, and he will have what he needs, as well.

Evaluating Returns From Income-Producing Property

In the story presented on pages 176 to 179, I contrast a cash-on-cash return with an overall return. If you're new to real estate investments and you're not familiar with these terms, it will be worth your while to pause a moment and learn how to properly evaluate the returns you anticipate receiving from any income-producing property, whether or not it's purchased through an LLC.

It is very easy to calculate a cash-on-cash return. To do so, simply divide the amount of cash your IRA is expected to receive from an investment in any given year by the amount that you invested. If, for instance, your IRA originally invested $25,000 and you receive a yearly return of $3,000, the cash-on-cash return is 12 percent ($3,000 ÷ $25,000 = .12).

The cash-on-cash return doesn't tell the whole story, though. To learn more, you must consider the project's overall return, which takes into consideration the equity buildup of your investment due to mortgage reduction and appreciation. The first concept, mortgage reduction, is easy to understand. As the mortgage is paid down, your equity in the project gets larger. Appreciation—an increase in the value of the property—is a bit more complicated. Appreciation can be affected by several different factors. Inflation, for instance, can affect apprecia-

THE UNRELATED BUSINESS INCOME TAX

If you read Chapter 4, you may remember the discussion of the Unrelated Business Income Tax (UBIT). (See page 75 for details.) This annual tax applies to income produced by IRA-purchased property that is mortgaged, or that incurred a mortgage with its acquisition. Included is property purchased with an LLC. The amount of the income subject to the UBIT is determined by the

tion. Changes in the surrounding neighborhood can also affect appreciation. If the neighborhood undergoes development, the value of the property goes up; if the neighborhood declines, so do property values. However, I feel that all of these factors result in inconsequential appreciation. In rare cases, these factors can have a great impact on a property's value, but a more significant effect is caused by the revenues generated by the project itself.

It's vital to realize that the value of any income-producing real estate investment is directly dependent on the amount of income it produces. That's why you have to pay particular attention to the income and expense numbers that are projected in the APOD and cash flow statements (see page 178). In addition you need to look at the leases that will be providing the income for the investments. Let's say that in Scenario 2, you read the leases and discover that each year, there is an automatic 3-percent increase in revenue. This means that your investment will increase in value by 3 percent a year. So, instead of the 12-percent return you calculated as your cash-on-cash return, you will receive a 15-percent return. If the mortgage is being repaid at another 3 percent per year, your return will actually be 18 percent because of your increase in equity.

Some people may feel that this is an oversimplification of the return analyses. However, years of experience have taught me that this is not the case. Rather, this is a tried-and-true method of analysis that you can use with confidence to choose the best income-producing investments for your IRA.

relationship between the amount of debt and the tax basis of the property.

To understand how the UBIT affects an LLC investment, let's return to the example of the retail park presented in Scenario 2. In the second year, the retail center has a 75-percent loan in relationship to the debt, and your income is $20,000—a 10-percent cash-on-cash return. How will the UBIT work? The first $1,000 of income is tax-free. The tax on the remaining $19,000 is based on the 75-percent relationship of loan to tax basis. Therefore, $14,250 is taxed—75 percent of the $19,000. If the tax rate were 37.5 percent, you would have to pay $5,343.75.

When the LLC-purchased property is sold, you will again have to pay the UBIT on your gain. In this case, however, your profit will be taxed at the lower capital gains rate. (For details, see page 78.)

This chapter has provided a glimpse of an incredible investment vehicle, the limited liability company. Through the LLC, you can make a myriad of high-return investments that can build IRA wealth faster than most people think is possible. Hopefully, this chapter has also provided a compelling glimpse of the many speculative investment opportunities that are out there, waiting to be found. In most areas, it is difficult to drive a mile without seeing a construction site or development. And at one point or another, every developer is in need of financing. Whether you look for these opportunities on your own or you enlist the aid of an expert real estate broker, your goal is to find a successful, stable developer with whom you can form a partnership that will benefit all involved.

Buying Yourself a Business

Success in business requires training and discipline and hard work. But if you're not frightened by these things, the opportunities are just as great today as they ever were.

—DAVID ROCKEFELLER (1915–   )

C an an IRA buy a business? Of course it can. Can it buy the company for which you work? Under certain circumstances, yes.

Right now, you may be wondering why the topic of buying a business is covered at all in a book whose main focus is on building your retirement fund through real estate investments. The answer is that very often, the purchase of a business encompasses the purchase of real estate. Consider, for instance, a restaurant that stands on its own lot. In a situation such as this, the property adds value to the business. Even if the restaurant failed, the real estate on which it stands would still have worth. In fact, in some cases, the property may be worth *more* than the business, and alone may justify your purchase of the enterprise. Whether or not an enterprise includes valuable land, though, if the business is profitable, its acquisition can dramatically increase your IRA wealth.

Just remember that this chapter has been included in the higher-risk portion of the book for a reason. When real estate or a note goes bad, you can usually recover because of the underlying security of the property. With a business, this is not always true. Consider the stock market adjustments of the past few years. Why did a lot of these stocks fall? Because they didn't have the equity they claimed to have. Businesses are not necessarily asset based. More often, they are cash-flow based. When the cash flow goes south, so does the business—unless it has assets to fall back on. So be careful, and before undertaking any enterprise, make sure to back your investment with thorough research and to surround yourself with a good crew. Buying a business can make your IRA flourish—but only if you do it right.

WHY BUY A BUSINESS?

Why would you want to purchase a business with your IRA? Perhaps the best answer is that the income from such an investment could be limitless. Consider the following true story of three entrepreneurs. Sometime ago, each of them used his Roth IRA funds to buy a $1,500 interest in their newly developed computer software company. Later, the three men sold the business for millions, putting the profits back into their Roth IRAs tax-free! Sure, these investors will still have to work day jobs until their retirement, but at least they won't have to work *for* their retirement. During their work years, they can spend everything they make. Their retirement years have been taken care of.

There are other reasons, too, to purchase a business. In these difficult times, for instance, employees sometimes find their companies failing through mismanagement, and their jobs disappearing along with the business itself. In certain cases, it is possible for employees to purchase a company, saving their jobs and the jobs of many other individuals. One of the scenarios presented in this chapter shows how this can be done. (See page 190.)

Whether you invest in a business purely to build IRA wealth or you are interested in saving a failing company, clearly, you should make such an investment only if the business is already profitable or if you know you can make it profitable. You are not looking for a loss here. For that reason, whenever possible, you'll want to seek out businesses with assets such as real estate or business-related equipment. These assets will hold their value even if the business fails.

YOUR CREW

Under no circumstances should you attempt to purchase a business without your crew onboard. Even if you've been working in the business in question for forty years and know it inside and out, you'll still need the help of qualified professionals.

When making most of the investments discussed in this book, the first crew member you need to consult is your real estate broker. But when you buy a business, you've probably moved out of your broker's area of expertise—unless, of course, your purchase involves real estate as well as the enterprise itself. In that case, you may want to use your broker to provide a separate evaluation of the property.

In most cases, your accountant will be an indispensable part of your crew. Before you buy a business, it is necessary to analyze the business's financial records, including two or three years of income and expense records. Most important are the expenses listed on the income tax statement. While statements of income are sometimes intentionally misleading, expense listings not only tend to be more accurate, but also provide a unique view of the company, showing if and how you can cut expenses to increase profitability. Unless you have considerable experience in this area and are well qualified to analyze these statements, definitely have your accountant crunch the numbers and give you a realistic appraisal of the company's strengths and weaknesses.

As you may expect, your attorney will provide invaluable assistance as you go about acquiring a business. You will want your purchase to exclude as many of the liabilities created by the previous owners as possible. You will also want to make sure that the company's contracts with other parties, including employees, are reviewed in detail for their merit. And you will want to insure that the structure of the purchase in no way runs afoul of IRS rules. These tasks require a good lawyer. However, the lawyer you used to buy a rental house is probably not the best choice when buying a business. Instead, you will want to find a good corporate lawyer who specializes in acquisitions. He will have the expertise needed to make this investment a success.

Will it be necessary to bring your title insurance company onboard? As you might expect, this will depend on whether the business includes real estate. If it does, the company will be needed to perform a title search and provide title insurance.

Buying a business may necessitate the addition of a new crew member—a business broker. In fact, if you are interested in buying a business but do not have a specific one in mind, a business broker should probably be the *first* crew member to bring onboard. In addition to informing you about businesses for sale, an experienced business broker can determine the value of a business, help decide if the purchase makes sense, and recommend appropriate terms for the sale. If you're in need of a broker, your best bet would be to get a recommendation from a friend. In the absence of such a recommendation, though, try contacting the International Business Brokers Association, Inc. (IBBA). (See the Resource List on page 223.) This nonprofit organization can steer you to an experienced broker in your area.

Finally, your IRA administrator will take care of the usual tasks, providing approval, arranging funding, and filing the necessary documents with the IRS. Because the purchase of a business is such a complex transaction, I highly recommend that once you, your accountant, and your attorney have structured the purchase, you run it past your administrator for approval. By doing this *before* any contracts have been signed—while changes in structure can still be made with relative ease—you may very well save yourself time, money, and aggravation.

MAKING THE PURCHASE

Purchasing a business is not too different from buying real estate. First, you must thoroughly research the prospective purchase, and make sure that the investment is a safe one that will add to your IRA wealth. Then, just as when you were buying property, you must choose the type of ownership desired—a limited liability company, for instance. And along the way, you must make sure to follow the rules provided by the IRS.

Earlier in this chapter, you learned how your attorney and accountant must research the company by examining its contracts and analyzing its financial records. Before we look at specific stories of business purchases, let's consider the other two elements just mentioned—the rules that govern your IRA's transactions with businesses, and the various ways you can structure the purchase.

Following the Rules

While there are a number of rules that govern the process of purchasing and conducting a business with your IRA, there are really just two major ones that you must remember. First, in most cases, you should not buy more than 49 percent of a business. Second, you cannot control the business in which you are investing. Let's briefly examine each of these regulations.

In Chapter 7, you learned that an IRA cannot invest with a "disqualified person." What I didn't mention in Chapter 7 is that a corporation can also be considered a disqualified person. This occurs when 50 percent or more of the business is owned by the IRA owner. Moreover, you and those family members who are considered "disqualified" should not own 50 percent or more of the stock combined. (For more information on disqualified people, see page 130.) Note that I said "should not" rather than "cannot." Why? Because it is not the 50-percent ownership itself that creates a prohibited transaction. Rather, a prohibited transaction is caused when there is 50-percent ownership by disqualified parties, and a transaction takes place between a disqualified party and the company. For instance, the business might borrow money from a member who is a disqualified party, or the business might acquire property in which one of the disqualified parties has an interest. In other words, in some cases, your IRA or a disqualified party *can* own 50 percent or more of the business, but because of the risks involved, this should usually be avoided. When would a larger percentage of ownership be an acceptable choice? Scenario 3 clarifies this rule by presenting a situation in which an IRA legitimately purchases a greater percentage of a business. (See page 192.)

Now, let's consider the rule that you cannot control the business in which you're investing. Specifically, the law states that the IRA account holder cannot have a "substantial interest" in the corporation, as such an interest would affect the account holder's best judgment. What does this mean in practice? It means that you cannot be an officer of the company in which your IRA owns shares. If you are found to run a significant portion of the company, your IRA's purchase of the company may be deemed a prohibited transaction—even if you own less than 50 percent of the business.

Structuring the Business

By now, you have probably realized that the business you buy with your IRA cannot be a sole proprietorship. IRS rules prohibit the IRA account holder from running the business. However, there are at least three ways in which you can structure your IRA investment in a business. The business can be a limited liability company (LLC), a limited partnership, or a C corporation. (An S corporation does not permit IRAs to be investors.)

Chapter 7 briefly discusses both the LLC and the limited partnership, and Chapter 9 explores the LLC in detail. If you want to learn about these partnerships, you'll find all the basics in these chapters.

The corporation is a different type of entity. The most common form of business organization, the *corporation* is a state-chartered business or organization formed by a group of people, and having rights and liabilities separate from those of the individuals involved. Like the members of an LLC, the members of a corporation are not liable for the corporation's debts. Therefore, while the assets of the company may be seized and sold, the assets of the investors cannot. However, the corporation is different from the LLC and limited partnership in that it can sell shares of easily transferable stock. Moreover, while the earnings of the LLC and limited partnership are taxed only once, those of the corporation are taxed twice. Income is first taxed at the corporate level using a corporate income tax rate. Then, distributions made to stockholders are taxed at the rates of the individual stockholders. Because of this double taxation, your returns may be lower. Of course, because you are investing in these businesses with your IRA rather than discretionary funds, all income will be tax-deferred or tax-exempt, depending on whether you're using a traditional or Roth IRA.

When determining the structure of your business, you will absolutely need to consult your attorney and accountant. All three structures just discussed provide the flexibility you need to make investments with your IRA. They even permit both your IRA and you, as well as other disqualified individuals, to invest in the same venture, as long as each member makes transactions only with the business and not with the other members. But to keep all transactions legal, you need to rely on a good crew. Hire qualified professionals, and heed their counsel as you choose the best business structure, and as you monitor all transactions to make sure they're in keeping with IRS codes.

You now are familiar with some of the basics of buying a business with your IRA. But you still may be wondering how, with all these rules and regulations, you can build IRA wealth through the purchase of a business. The following scenarios will show you just how profitable these investments can be.

Buying a Business—Scenario 1

Let's say that the owner of a manufacturing business has asked you to invest in his business. It is a small company with a net worth of around $500,000, and he needs $200,000 to buy more equipment for the expansion of his plant. The business is held as a corporation. The owner is the president, and he and his family are the only stockholders. You call in your accountant to audit the business, and he decides that it is a good risk. The business, he says, is actually profiting by over $70,000 per year. With new equipment, it can do even better.

There are two basic ways in which your IRA can invest in the manufacturing company. The first and most obvious way to invest is to loan the money to the corporation. The second is to buy shares in the corporation—to become an owner. Your accountant tells you that if you were to loan the money at a 10-percent return, your IRA would receive $20,000 a year in interest. While this is a healthy return, no matter how well the business did, your profit would always remain the same. If, however, you used the money to buy shares, you would own 40 percent of the company, and would be entitled to $28,000 per year (.40 × $70,000 profit = $28,000). Moreover, your return would increase as the company grew. You choose to buy shares.

It's time to bring in your attorney. He reviews the current structure of the corporation to see if there are any red flags, and to determine if any changes must be made in corporate documents to allow the shift from a family-run operation to one with outside shareholders. Since your attorney finds no problems, you're ready to make the purchase. You send a direction letter to your IRA administrators, and they buy the shares.

You now own 40 percent of the company, with a yearly income of $28,000. As the company grows, so does your income. What if you later decide that you need the money to fund another investment—or to fund your actual retirement? At any point, you can simply sell your shares and put the money back into your IRA. If you used a Roth IRA, you will never have to pay taxes on the income. If you used a traditional account, all gains will be tax-deferred.

Buying a Business—Scenario 2

Let's say that you have worked for a franchised widget company for the past fifteen years. All of the other franchises are out on the West Coast, but yours was an experiment—an attempt to break into the East Coast market. For the first ten years, when the parent company paid attention to your manufacturing plant, the franchise did well. Then the parent company lost interest and failed to spend the money needed to modernize the equipment. Over the past five years or so, you have seen the business going downhill, mainly because of neglect.

Realizing that it's only a matter of time before the parent company closes the plant, you pull the key employees together to discuss your options. One, of course, is to cut and run, moving your 401(k) money to your next employer and developing a new bunch of friends and colleagues. But you work with a great crew and don't want to start over. The accountant for your franchise explains what went wrong, and what it would take to get the plant back on its feet. You talk to the floor managers, salespeople, and engineers, and a plan is created to save the firm.

To make the company viable, two things must occur. Several unprofitable lines must be dropped, and new equipment must be purchased so that you can successfully compete in the marketplace. You take the plan to the CEO of your parent company, and he promises to get back to you about your proposal. Of course he never does. He's already planning the shutdown.

You call another meeting with your group and tell them, "Let's just buy the company ourselves." You've all been at the plant for many years and have done well. Although none of you has the horsepower to pull off a buy-out on your own, you explain that if you pooled the assets of all of the members of the core group, you just might be able to make the purchase.

After several strategic sessions with an accountant and an attorney, the plan is formed. It's decided that you will wait until the inevitable phone call from the CEO to pull the rabbit out of the hat. However, you'll go ahead and prepare the rabbit now. The strategy is this: Your group is going to combine its 401(k) assets with discretionary funds, and buy the company! No, you can't self-direct your 401(k) funds. But when the axe falls, you will each have the option of rolling your 401(k) into self-directed IRAs. There are substantial assets in the 401(k) now, because the average employee has been contributing for more than twelve years. If you combine that with the discretionary money that several of you have socked away, and you add a small loan from the bank, there should be enough not only to purchase the company, but also to update the plant and make it profitable.

Your attorney advises you to form a limited liability company to accommodate the IRA funds and discretionary money. Each contributing party will buy shares in the LLC according to the amount he has to invest, taking shares both for his IRA and himself. The group chooses the attorney as the managing member of the LLC, since an IRA cannot manage itself. If one of the individual members took control, he might be deemed a disqualified person and void the investment.

The attorney creates another corporation for the future ownership and management of the company. This company hires a CPA firm to oversee and manage its affairs. The attorney is also the president of this corporation.

When the CEO of the parent company calls to say they're shutting down the plant, you're ready. Immediately, you tell him that you would like to purchase the company. Since he is about to shut it down anyway, you are able to negotiate a very good price. The employees are terminated, and they roll over their 401(k) assets into individual self-directed IRAs.

As planned, the employees use both their IRAs and their savings to purchase membership interests in the LLC, being careful not to allow any one person's IRA or personal investment to reach 50 percent ownership. The LLC buys the corporation with the management company in place, which in turn buys the company and all of its stock. The management company hires back the employees who arranged the purchase, and together, you implement the needed changes. The company thrives, and dividends from the ownership of the corporation are paid to both the IRAs and the individuals. Everyone is happy.

Buying a Business—Scenario 3

Let's say that you just got laid off from your job of fifteen years because of that nemesis known as corporate downsizing. Translated, that means, "Let's get rid of all of the high-paid employees and keep the ones that cost less." The good news is that you have been an active participant in your company's 401(k) plan, and you have a nice nest egg of $700,000. The bad news is that you are now fifty-five years old, and nobody wants to pay for the kind of experience you bring to the table. You decide, "To heck with them. I'll just go out and buy a job."

You put the word out that you are interested in purchasing a business. Casually, you let your real estate broker know, because he is always out and about, and may find something by accident. In addition, you routinely scan the newspapers under "Business for Sale." One day, you notice that a number of listings were made by a business broker named Buy Your Business Here. Although none of the listings looks interesting, you decide to call the broker and see what else he has to offer. When you contact the broker, instead of telling you what he has, he asks tough questions about the type of business you want. What kind of experience do you have? What kind of return are you looking for? Do you enjoy working with employees? You decide to visit the broker, who promptly gives you a form to fill out so that he can determine what will suit you best. After much consultation, the broker and you realize that you're not really looking for a job. What you want is security and a fair wage. You really don't want to run a business, but you do want to receive cash flow and to build wealth as you go. The business broker now has what he needs to locate a business that will be a good fit. Best of all, just like a real estate broker, he will do the job at no cost to you. His fee will be paid by the seller of the business.

After several weeks go by, the business broker gives you a call. He has found a business that he thinks will meet your needs. The owner of a dry cleaning plant retired several years ago, and for the last five years, a management staff has been running the plant for him. Now he is moving to another state, and he wants to divest himself of his local assets. In completing his due diligence, the broker has gathered the business's tax returns and balance sheets for the last five years, as well as a current profit and loss statement. He has also obtained an inventory of equipment, and a current environment level-one statement made by an independent contractor who examined the property for environmental hazards. The equipment is relatively new, and the property is clean. So far, so good.

The seller is asking $495,000 for the business and the real estate on which it stands. The tax records show that he has been enjoying an average income from the business of about $50,000 per year, with a high of $58,000 and a low of $40,000. The low occurred five years ago, and he explains that at the time, he was trying to find a decent manager for the plant. You know how to divide, and you determine that the return on the investment would be about 10 percent. ($50,000 ÷ $495,000 = .10)

Now it's time to get your real estate broker involved. To get a sense of the property's value, you have your broker look at comparable sales. The building itself is approximately 5,000 square feet, and sits on two lots of 7,500 square feet each. The extra lot is used for employee parking—which is probably not the best use of the property, as there are only five employees. Your real estate broker finds that the land values are $5 per square foot, while the value of the building is about $300,000. So the total value of the real estate alone is $375,000. This means that you will be paying $125,000 for the business and the equipment. You interview the manager, and you like what you see. She has lived in the community for twenty years, she enjoys her job, and she has every intention of staying on if you want her.

It's time to make the purchase. The accountant and attorney work together to draft the purchase agreement. Because you want to develop the real estate separately, you decide to allocate a certain amount of the purchase price to the real estate and a certain amount to the equipment and business, for a combined total of $495,000. The real estate will be purchased directly by the IRA, and the business will be purchased through a limited liability company. Your IRA will own 90 percent of the business, and the other 10 percent will be given to the manager as an incentive bonus. At this point, you might be wondering if this violates the 50-percent rule discussed on page 187. As mentioned in that earlier discussion, this rule has its exceptions. In this case, as long as the disqualified parties do not do additional business together, the transaction will not be considered prohibited.

You obtain title insurance on the real estate, and have the title company submit the paperwork to your IRA administrator with a direction letter. Both the company and the property are yours.

When the dust settles, you have real estate holdings worth $375,000, and an ongoing business that provides a $50,000 annual cash flow. Moreover, you have an extra lot that can be further developed, leased, or sold. In other words, you now have two potential profit centers instead of just one. If and when the LLC sells the business, your IRA will still own the real property, including any improvements that have been made over the years.

The scenarios in this chapter have sketched out only a few ways in which you can purchase a business with your IRA. There are many, many more ways in which this can be accomplished. If you can imagine it, you can probably do it. And as long as you thoroughly research the business and follow the rules set down by the IRS, your retirement account and the business you acquire can grow together by leaps and bounds.

PART FOUR

Your Retirement

If you have read the previous chapters, you know how IRA wealth can be created through well-researched investments in real estate. When will you be able to start enjoying the fruits of your labor? That's what the next chapter, "Evaluating Your Choices," is all about.

As you might expect, different people find themselves in different situations as they approach retirement. While some must rely heavily on their IRA for daily living expenses, and may want to start withdrawing money from their account long before they retire, others have little or no need to draw upon their IRAs even after their working years have ended. However, the Internal Revenue Service has set down specific rules to govern Individual Retirement Accounts, and these rules affect not only the investments you can make with your IRA, but also when you can begin to pull assets out of your account. Chapter 11 discusses these IRS rules, and also provides guidelines for modifying your investments as you approach retirement. It even tells you how to prepare for the inevitable by naming your IRA beneficiary, so that your family can continue to benefit from your retirement account after you're gone.

Before you turn to the last chapter of *IRA Wealth*, an important caution is in order. As you near your retirement years, you may be tempted to cash in all your IRA investments. Don't! Why would you want your profits to sit inactive in your account, waiting to be depleted? You worked hard for your money, and you want it to continue working hard for you. By making carefully chosen real estate investments throughout the course of your retirement, you'll be able to keep your IRA robust and healthy, supporting you and your family as you enjoy all the pleasures that life has to offer.

Evaluating Your Choices

It is better to have a permanent income
than to be fascinating.

—OSCAR WILDE (1854–1900)

Throughout your working life, you wisely set aside a portion of your income and made careful investments as a means of preparing for your retirement. Now retirement is drawing near, and if you're like most people, a number of questions are beginning to arise in your mind. How soon can you begin taking money out of your IRA? Do you have enough money in your IRA to meet your needs in the coming years? Can you, if you wish, allow your money to remain in your IRA and grow?

This chapter was designed to answer many important questions about using your IRA during your retirement years. The chapter begins by filling you in on the IRS rules that govern disbursements. It then helps you assess your financial situation and determine if your income will, in fact, be adequate. Finally, it guides you in making any changes needed to insure that your golden years are financially secure, and in making provisions for your spouse or other loved ones.

As you read the following pages, keep in mind that the IRS rules which govern IRA disbursements are complex. This chapter presents only the basics so that you can start evaluating your investments and modifying your strategies as necessary. For more detailed information and guidance, you'll want to consult your financial planner, accountant, and attorney.

UNDERSTANDING THE IRS RULES ON DISTRIBUTIONS

Before you consider changing your IRA investments in preparation for retirement, it's important to understand the IRS rules for making distributions. While you can begin pulling money out of your IRA at any time, if you do so before the age of 59½, the government will impose a penalty. So let's look first at the rules that affect early distributions. Following that, we'll look at the rules that govern distributions made during your retirement.

Early Distributions

Because the government does not want you to benefit from tax-deferred and tax-free retirement plans prior to your retirement years, in most cases, it imposes penalties to discourage early withdrawal. If you take a distribution from your traditional IRA prior to age 59½, state and federal income tax will, of course, be assessed against your withdrawal, as your distribution will be considered ordinary income by the IRS in the year you withdraw it. In addition, a 10-percent penalty will be imposed on the net amount withdrawn. If you take a distribution from a Roth IRA prior to age 59½, or if you do so before the account has been in existence for five years, the earnings will also be subject to a 10-percent premature distribution penalty, as well as state and federal income tax on the earned portion of the distribution.

Fortunately for the account holder in need, though, there are exceptions to the above rules. These exceptions are as follows:

❏ In the event of the IRA account holder's death, a distribution can be made to a beneficiary or estate without penalty, even if the account holder was not 59½ at the time of death. However, if the account holder's spouse elects to treat the IRA as her own by becoming the new account holder, she must wait until age 59½ to make penalty-free withdrawals. (For more information on an IRA beneficiary's options, see page 208.)

❏ If the account holder is unable to engage in substantially gainful activity due to disability, withdrawals can be made without penalty.

❏ If the account holder's medical expenses are above and beyond 7.5 percent of his adjusted gross income, withdrawals can be made without penalty to cover those expenses. Penalty-free withdrawals can also be made to pay health insurance premiums as long as the account holder is unemployed.

❏ Under certain circumstances, penalty-free withdrawals can be made to cover the educational expenses of the account holder or the account holder's spouse, child, or grandchild.

❏ Penalty-free transfers can be made directly from the account holder's IRA to the divorced spouse's IRA. If, however, the money is withdrawn and paid as cash, the withdrawal will be penalized.

❏ If the account holder has not owned a home within the past two years, he can withdraw up to $10,000 penalty-free to purchase a home for himself or his spouse, child, grandchild, parent, or spouse's parent. Indeed, the account holder and his spouse can each withdraw $10,000 from their respective accounts, for a total of $20,000—as long as all the money will be used to purchase the same house.

❏ If distributions are made as a series of equal periodic payments calculated to exhaust the IRA over the account holder's expected lifetime or the joint lives of the account holder and his spouse, the withdrawals will be penalty-free.

Before you make an early withdrawal that you believe will be penalty-free, by all means discuss it with your accountant. He will be able to determine if the early distribution is a legitimate exception, or will be penalized by the IRS.

Distributions Made During Retirement

Once you turn 59½, you can make withdrawals from your IRA in any amount you wish. Once you turn 70½, the rules regarding distributions vary according to the type of IRA you are using. If you have a traditional IRA, you are actually *required by law* to make minimum distributions. If, however, you have your money in a Roth IRA, you can leave your assets in the account for as long as you wish. Mandatory lifetime distribution rules do not apply to the Roth IRA.

Mandatory distributions of traditional IRA assets must begin by April 1 of the year following the year in which you reach age 70½. These distributions can be made in one of three basic ways:

1. You can make a lump-sum distribution, meaning that you can withdraw all your assets at once.

2. You can purchase an annuity contract from an insurance company, which will pay out the IRA funds to you according to a set schedule. People often use annuities to avoid the risk of running out of money during their lifetime. Be aware, though, that if you pass away before all the payments are made, the unexpended funds will not go to your beneficiary, but will be used to pay those annuitants who live longer.

3. You can take out minimum yearly distributions in accordance with either the IRS Uniform Lifetime Table or the IRS Joint Life and Last Survivor Expectancy table, depending upon your situation.

Both of the tables used to calculate minimum distributions are based on your age and the age of any beneficiary—usually, your spouse. Younger people, who have a greater life expectancy, are required to receive smaller yearly amounts so that their account will not be exhausted during their lifetime. As people age and life expectancy declines, minimum distributions become larger.

If you choose to make minimum distributions, and your spouse is less than ten years younger than you *or* you are unmarried, you must use the Uniform Lifetime Table to calculate your required minimum distribution (RMD). To do so, first note the IRA balance you had at the end of the previous calendar year. Remember that if you have several traditional IRA accounts, your balance will be the total of the separate balances. Then turn to Table 11.1, and find the divisor that corresponds to your age. Divide the account balance by the divisor, and you'll have the required minimum distribution for the current year. For instance, if you had $500,000 in your IRA at the end of last year, and you are now eighty years of age, your RMD for this year is $26,737.96. ($500,000 ÷ 18.7 = $26,737.96.)

If you are married and your spouse is ten or more years younger than you, you must use the Joint Life and Last Survivor Expectancy table found in IRS Publication 590. You can order this publication by mail, or you can find it on the Internal Revenue Service website by using the "Search Forms and Publications for" feature. (See the Resource List on page 224.) Once you have the table in hand, it's fairly simple to calculate your RMD. First, find your divisor at the intersection of the column containing your age and the row containing the age of your spouse. Then divide your account balance at the end of the previous calendar year by the divisor, and you'll have your required minimum distribution for the current year.

Naturally, you can take penalty-free distributions greater than the minimum at any time, as long as you are age 59½ or older. However, if you have a traditional IRA and you fail to make the minimum distribution, a 50-percent tax will be levied on the minimum amount that should have been distributed that year.

Finally, be aware that distribution rules change all the time. That's why it's so important to work with a good accountant, who will make sure that your IRA distributions are in line with current regulations.

AS YOU APPROACH RETIREMENT

As you just learned, you need make no distributions from your IRA until you reach age 70½. But if you have a traditional IRA account, you should take a hard look at your IRA assets a few

TABLE 11.1. UNIFORM LIFETIME TABLE			
AGE OF ACCOUNT HOLDER	**DIVISOR**	**AGE OF ACCOUNT HOLDER**	**DIVISOR**
70	27.4	93	9.6
71	26.5	94	9.1
72	25.6	95	8.6
73	24.7	96	8.1
74	23.8	97	7.6
75	22.9	98	7.1
76	22.0	99	6.7
77	21.2	100	6.3
78	20.3	101	5.9
79	19.5	102	5.5
80	18.7	103	5.2
81	17.9	104	4.9
82	17.1	105	4.5
83	16.3	106	4.2
84	15.5	107	3.9
85	14.8	108	3.7
86	14.1	109	3.4
87	13.4	110	3.1
88	12.7	111	2.9
89	12.0	112	2.6
90	11.4	113	2.4
91	10.8	114	2.1
92	10.2	115 and over	1.9

years before your minimum distributions must begin to see if any adjustments must be made in your investment plan.

Don't examine your account alone—especially if your IRA investments are varied. Instead, enlist the help of your financial planner, who has been keeping an eye on your investment strategies over the years, and your accountant. Between the two, you should be able to get the advice you need to make any necessary adjustments.

Keep in mind that while you may need to increase liquidity to meet IRS regulations, you also have to consider growth. Many investors don't realize that they can keep building their retirement accounts even after they stop working. As soon as retirement comes into view, their first thought is to cash in their investments. However, it makes no sense to let your money stagnate if you can make it work for you. Moreover, if you're like many retirees, you will have to keep making wise investments to insure that your assets are not depleted, but will continue to provide you with necessary income.

When you sit down to evaluate your IRA investments, you will first have to consider the income you will receive during retirement. Then, you will have to determine how much income you will actually require. To clarify this, let's assume that you will have the following sources of income, including your IRA:

INCOME SOURCES	MONTHLY INCOME	ANNUAL INCOME
Social Security	$1,500	$18,000
Rental House Held by IRA	$1,000	$12,000
Spousal Pension Plan	$1,200	$14,400
Total	$3,700	$44,400

Let's assume that when you add up your estimated costs, you find that you will need $5,000 a month—$60,000 annually—just to exist during your retirement years. When you compare this with your expected income, you discover that you have a $15,600 annual shortfall. You need another $1,300 a month.

Now that you know what you need, you take a look at your IRA, which contains $500,000, but includes no income-producing investments other than the rental property. What type of investment can you make to generate the additional income you need, and yet build your account?

If you invest $150,000 in a 12-percent note, you will receive $1,500 per month, and your income will be sufficiently increased without tapping into your principal. But let's say that you also want to travel, which will mean added expenses of $20,000 a year. You could purchase additional notes to generate that income, or you could invest an additional $200,000 in an LLC that provides a cash dividend of 10 percent annually. The difference between the notes and the LLC is that the notes will provide the income you need, but will not build your assets, while over the years, the LLC will provide increased equity through rent increases and mortgage reduction. Therefore, your shares will also grow in value, building further IRA wealth.

If you have used your IRA to purchase a residence for your retirement years, be sure to budget in the cost of taking that as a disbursement, because that property will have to be in your name—not the IRA's—by the time you move into it. These disbursements can be handled in a couple of ways. First, you can take the property as a one-time disbursement. If you used a traditional IRA, you will have to pay income tax on that disbursement, though, so check with your accountant to see if that would be feasible. If the tax hit is going to be too great, consider your second option—taking partial disbursements over a period of three or four years. Say that you are planning to move into your retirement home at age sixty-three. You can disburse a third of the asset in your sixtieth year, a third in your sixty-first year, and a third in your sixty-second year. That way, you will pay only a third of the taxes each year. How will you make these disbursements? For a few years, you and your IRA will have tenancy-in-common ownership of the dwelling, with the interests gradually transferring from the IRA to you until all of the interests are in your name. (For information on tenancy-in-common ownership, see page 71 of Chapter 4.)

WHEN YOU REACH AGE 70½

As you've already learned, if you have a traditional IRA, once you retire, you will have to start taking out at least minimum distributions from your account on a yearly basis. These distributions will be mandatory even if you continue to work.

When you reach retirement age, your IRA administrator will provide you with an information statement which specifies when your minimum distributions must start. The administrator will also provide this information to the IRS. The IRA administrator will not, however, report the amount of the minimum distribution to the IRS—only that a distribution is required.

As you may have already realized, you don't have to take your required distribution in cash. You can also take it as real property—or, for that matter, as any security or other investment. When you use these assets as disbursements, you basically change them from IRA assets to your own personal assets. So liquidity may not be the problem you thought it would be.

Of course, if you have made your investments with a Roth IRA, you will not be required to take *any* distributions from your account. In fact, as long as you have earned income, you will even be permitted to make additional contributions to your Roth!

PLANNING FOR THE INEVITABLE

Although we all hate to think about it, the fact is that death is inevitable. And any financial plans—including those involving your IRA—must include planning for the inevitable.

Many people give little thought to the beneficiary they named when they first opened their IRA. They believe that their will is going to determine who inherits all their assets, including their retirement fund. However, a will does not necessarily override the beneficiary designation made in an IRA. That's why it's so vital to name a beneficiary.

Any legally competent person or entity can be your IRA beneficiary. You can, for example, name your spouse, child, grandchild, or friend; or a trust or charity. It is also possible to name multiple beneficiaries. Be aware, though, that when more than one person has been named, the age of the eldest will be used to determine your required minimum distribution during your lifetime. In other words, in the case of multiple beneficiaries, you may not be able to use your spouse in RMD calculations. In addition, if your spouse is one of the beneficiaries, he or she may lose some privileges that would have been afforded if no other beneficiaries had been named. For this reason, account holders often choose to name their spouse as their sole primary beneficiary, and their children or grandchildren as contingent beneficiaries, meaning that they will receive the proceeds of the IRA only if the primary beneficiary predeceases the account holder. This arrangement allows the account holder to use his spouse in the RMD calculations, and permits the spouse to benefit from the advantages afforded to a sole spousal beneficiary. Finally, keep in mind that if your state has community property laws, you may need the consent of your spouse to name a nonspousal beneficiary.

Once a beneficiary inherits your IRA, her options will be determined by her relationship to you. Your spouse will have the greatest number of options. She will be able to treat it as her own IRA by designating herself as the account holder; to treat it as her own by rolling it into her own retirement plan; or to treat it as an inheritance and take distributions. Any beneficiary other than your spouse, however, will not be allowed to treat the IRA as her own. Instead, she simply must take either a complete distribution or a series of distributions. If your money is held in a traditional IRA, the beneficiary will have to pay taxes on the distributions. If you have a Roth IRA, the distributions will be tax-free.

Your financial planner and/or your attorney can help you review your situation and choose the beneficiary or beneficiaries that would make the most sense in your circumstances. Should you wish to change your beneficiary at any time, you need only contact your IRA administrator.

Whether you are nearing retirement or are already enjoying your golden years, it's important to continue making wise investments to increase your retirement wealth. As you've seen, smart investments—backed, of course, by real estate—can do far more that make your retirement pleasurable and secure. They can also help you insure the long-term financial welfare of your spouse, your children, and your grandchildren—even after you're gone.

Conclusion

What better to invest in than your future?

—PATRICK W. RICE

In my many years of guiding people's financial growth, I've discovered that those who take the time and energy to understand the principles of real estate investment—the very principles outlined in this book—are the ones who usually wind up with retirement riches. *IRA Wealth* provides you with the essentials you need to start investing your retirement funds in ways you may never have known were possible. You now understand how it's done, so start doing it! Procrastination will only slow the growth of your IRA.

The reality is that some of you will put this knowledge to use, and some of you will simply find this interesting reading. If you are one of the people who chooses to create wealth for your retirement, let me be the first to congratulate you. If you are a young investor, I am truly excited. By following the guidelines in this book, you will create retirement wealth that your parents never imagined was possible. For those who are older, feel confident that you can still substantially improve your position and enjoy a secure retirement.

First and foremost, put your crew together, selecting your crew members carefully. Then put your oars in the water and start moving towards your goal. Plot your course, embarking first on small ventures until you get your sea legs. Then keep making adjustments to maximize the distance you can go in a day. At each step, consult your crew to determine if you're still on course. If something doesn't work—if you find yourself moving away from instead of toward your objective—stop. But don't give up. Regroup and set another course. Successful investors aren't successful because they've avoided making mistakes. Rather, they've been able to learn from their mistakes and continually choose wiser investments.

Most investors have discovered that the stock market often isn't the solution to their financial problems. Stocks go up and down. The key to financial security has always been diversification, but this strategy doesn't work if you simply buy shares in different commodities. True diversification comes from identifying investments that are independent of the market's ups and downs. This may be hard to accept in a world in which so many advertisements constantly push us to invest our money in stocks and bonds, and deftly steer us towards banks and brokerage houses. It may seem safer to stick with what's known. My answer to this is that recent history has shown just how *unsafe* standard investments can be. On the other hand, my experience with thousands of clients has shown that real estate investments—when wisely made, as detailed in this book—can build your IRA while keeping your retirement money safe and secure.

If you would like to know more about the subject of this book, feel free to visit my website at www.iraresource.com. This site provides a wealth of information about self-directed IRAs, as well as about investing IRA funds in real estate. Moreover, it will allow you to sign up for my newsletter, a monthly publication that will keep you abreast of IRA news and provide helpful investment tips. Tools like this can be invaluable as you build your retirement fund.

This book has been a great pleasure to write. Hopefully, within its pages, you have found both the inspiration and the information needed to start building IRA wealth. See you on the cruise ship line!

Glossary

All words that appear in *italic type* are defined within the glossary.

abstract of title. A historical summary of a property's *title* that goes back to the first owner. This type of *title report*—used mainly in the so-called abstract states found on the East Coast and in the Midwest—is prepared by the buyer's attorney.

agreement of sale. See *contract of sale.*

"and or assigns." See *assign.*

annuity. Any investment that generates a series of regular payments guaranteed to continue for a specified period of time.

appreciation. The increase in a property's value due to a number of factors, including *inflation,* decreased taxes, an increased demand for land or housing, increased income, and modernization of the property itself or of the surrounding neighborhood.

asking price. The list price that the seller would like to receive for a property.

assign. To transfer certain rights, including property rights, to another party. When a *contract of sale* or purchase agreement includes your name followed by "and or assigns," it allows you to transfer ownership of the contract to your IRA.

attach. To legally seize property in order to force payment of a debt.

balloon payment. A final loan payment that is greater than the installment payments that preceded it, and pays the loan in full.

beneficiary. The person who is designated to receive the benefits—cash, property, etc.—of an IRA account after the death of the account holder.

blanket mortgage. A single *mortgage* that covers more than one piece of property.

cash flow. The periodic income available to an investor after all periodic expenses have been paid. For instance, the cash flow of a rental apartment would be computed by subtracting expenditures such as taxes and utilities (the money going out) from the rent (the money coming in).

cash-on-cash return. A measure of the profitability of an income-producing property, expressed as a percentage. To calculate the cash-on-cash return of an investment, divide the amount of cash received from the property in a given year by the amount originally invested.

certificate of deposit (CD). A type of savings account in which a specified sum of money is deposited for a set period of time, yielding a return that is generally higher than that of a passbook-type savings account.

closing. The event that transfers ownership of a property from the seller to the buyer in accordance with the *contract of sale*. Generally, the buyer, seller, lender (if any), and their agents are present at the closing.

collateral. Property pledged as security for a debt. If the debt is not repaid in accordance with the terms of the *security instrument*—the *mortgage* or *deed of trust*—the borrower risks losing the property.

commercial property. Real estate intended for use by a retail, wholesale, office, hotel, or service business. Properties deemed commercial include hotels and motels, apartment houses, resorts, restaurants, service stations, convenience stores, shopping centers, and office buildings.

compound interest. *Interest* paid on both the *principal* and any unpaid accumulated interest of previous periods. See also *simple interest.*

condominium. An individual unit in a multi-unit attached residential or commercial structure, in which the individual units are owned privately, and any commonly used areas such as sidewalks are owned jointly.

consideration. See *option consideration.*

contract of sale. A written agreement between the buyer and the owner of a piece of property, in which the buyer agrees to buy the property and the owner agrees to sell as long as certain conditions are satisfied. This is also called an agreement of sale and a purchase agreement.

contract rent. The rent of a unit such as an apartment as stated in the lease. See also *market rent.*

corporation. A state-chartered business or organization, formed by an individual or by a group of people, and having rights and liabilities separate from those of the individuals involved. The corporation is characterized by the limited liability of its owners; the issuance of freely transferable shares; centralized management; and the fact that it can exist indefinitely, beyond the lifetimes of any members or founders.

Coverdell Education Savings Account. See *Education IRA.*

credit report. An evaluation of an individual's history of debt repayment and/or capacity to repay debt.

deed of trust. A legal document, used in some states instead of a *mortgage,* that pledges property to secure the repayment of a loan. A deed of trust vests the *title* of the property in one or several trustees to secure the loan's payment.

defect in title. Any legal document, such as a *lien,* that makes the ownership of a property subject to a competing claim.

developed land. See *improved land.*

developer. An individual or company that makes a business of transforming *raw land* into *improved land* through the use of capital and labor.

discount. The difference between the current balance of a promissory *note* or other obligation and the amount actually paid for the note.

discounted note. A promissory *note* sold for less than its current balance.

discretionary funds. Any money that remains from net income after essential living expenses have been paid.

down payment. The portion of the purchase price of a property that the buyer pays in cash rather than financing with a *mortgage.*

due diligence. A careful study performed of the physical, financial, legal, and social characteristics of a specific piece of property, and of its predicted investment performance.

Education IRA. An *Individual Retirement Account* created exclusively to pay the qualified educational expenses of the designated beneficiary of the account. This is more formally referred to as the Coverdell Education Savings Account.

encumbrance. Anything, such as a *mortgage* or tax, that complicates the title process and affects the value or use of a property.

equity. The interest or value that an owner has in property over and above any debt incurred.

equity investor. An individual who has purchased partial ownership of a property by supplying cash rather than expertise.

escrow. Money and documents deposited with a third party, called an *escrow agent*, to be delivered upon the fulfillment of conditions stipulated in a *contract of sale*.

escrow agent. An individual or company that receives *escrow* for deposit or delivery. In some states, the *title insurance company* most often serves as the escrow agent. In other states, an attorney typically holds the escrow.

face value. The value of a promissory *note* at its creation. See also *note balance*.

foreclosure. The legal process whereby a borrower who has failed to make *mortgage* payments is deprived of his interest in the mortgaged property. This usually involves a forced sale of the property, the proceeds of which are used to pay the mortgage debt.

foreclosure sale. The public sale of a mortgaged property following *foreclosure*. The proceeds of the sale are used to pay the *mortgage* debt, with any excess going to the mortgagor (the property owner).

handyman's special. A house that requires extensive remodeling and repairs, and, as a result, sells for a relatively low price.

hard equity. A contribution to the construction of property in the form of cash rather than labor or services. See also *soft equity*.

improved land. Land that has been partly or fully developed for use through the addition of utilities, landscaping, roads, or buildings. This is also known as developed land.

Individual Retirement Account (IRA). A personal retirement account, also referred to as an Individual Retirement Arrangement, that an individual can establish by making yearly contributions which are limited in amount. Various types of IRAs are available, each with its own rules. See also *Education IRA; Roth IRA; traditional IRA.*

inflation. 1. An increase in price levels. **2.** A loss in the purchasing power of money.

infrastructure. Basic public works such as roads, sewers, water systems, drainage systems, and utilities.

interest. The cost of borrowing or otherwise using money, expressed as a rate, such as 6 percent. Depending on the way it is calculated, interest can be either simple or compound. See *compound interest; simple interest.*

IRA. See *Individual Retirement Account.*

IRA administrator. In this book, a company that has responsibility for the operation of a *self-directed IRA.* The administrator reviews the documentation of each investment vehicle; compiles the paperwork necessary for each transaction; files the paperwork with the IRS; and holds cash, *title* to properties, and all other assets of the account.

Joint Life and Last Survivor Expectancy table. The table created by the IRS to calculate *required minimum distributions* when an IRA account holder is age 70½ or older, and married to someone who is ten or more years younger.

judgment. The decision of a court in a civil action, stating that one individual is indebted to another, and fixing the amount of the debt. For instance, if a renter fails to pay rent, the landlord can obtain a judgment from the court against the renter.

judgment creditor. The individual or entity who has received a *judgment* for money due from a *judgment debtor.*

judgment debtor. The individual or entity against whom a *judgment* has been issued.

Keogh plan. A type of retirement plan for self-employed individuals, small business owners, and members of partnerships.

land sale contract. A legal document, used in some states instead of a *mortgage,* which passes the ownership (*title*) of a property to the buyer only after the contract has been paid in full. This is also called a real estate contract.

lien. A legal claim that one person has on the property of another person as security for a debt. A *mortgage,* for example, is considered a lien.

life estate. The right to use or occupy a property that expires upon the death of the owner and/or another specified person, such as the owner's spouse.

limited liability company (LLC). A combination of a *corporation* and a partnership in which each party buys shares in the LLC according to the funds he has available. Like a corporation, the LLC offers personal liability to each of the parties involved so that members can't lose more money than they contributed. Like a partnership, earnings are taxed only once. The LLC is used to hold title to and manage real estate or a business.

limited partnership. A form of ownership in which there are two types of partners: limited partners and general partners. Limited partners provide financial backing, but have little role in the management of the property and no personal liability for its debts. General partners are responsible for managing the property, and have unlimited personal liability. Like *limited liability companies,* limited partnerships allow each party to buy shares in a property according to the funds he has available.

list price. See *asking price.*

loan-to-value ratio (LTV). The relationship between the amount of money borrowed on a property and the value of the property. A loan with a lower loan-to-value ratio—in other words, a loan in which the amount borrowed is smaller relative to the property's value—involves less risk than a loan with a higher ratio, because the borrower has more *equity* in the property, and therefore more reason to repay the loan.

manufactured home. See *mobile home.*

market price. The actual price paid for a piece of property. Note that this is different from *market value.*

market rent. The rent that a comparable rental unit—a similar house, for instance—would command if offered on the market. See also *contract rent.*

market value. An estimation of the price that could be obtained for a piece of property on the current market.

mobile home. A residential unit manufactured in a factory and designed for transport to a permanent site, such as a mobile home park or a mobile home subdivision. This is also known as a manufactured home.

money market account. A type of savings account that invests funds in money market instruments, such as United States Treasury bills, *certificates of deposit*, and commercial paper.

mortgage. A legal document that pledges property to a lender as security for payment of a debt. The mortgage is used in only some states. In other states, a *deed of trust* or *land sale contract* is used instead.

nonrecourse loan. A type of loan structured so that if the loan isn't paid back as promised, the lender may take the property to satisfy the debt, but may not take any of the borrower's other assets, such as his car.

note. An unrecorded legal document that obligates the borrower to repay a debt, such as a *mortgage* loan, at a stated *interest* rate during a specified period of time. This is also called a promissory note.

note balance. The amount remaining to be paid on a promissory *note*. See also *face value*.

offer. A verbal or written statement of the buyer's interest in purchasing a property at a specified price. A verbal offer is never legally binding. In some states, however, a written offer is binding, while in others, it is not.

one-hundred-percent location. A site that is far superior to other sites in the area due to a commanding view, unusually good access, or other factors. Because it's the "best" site, land values and rents are normally highest in that area.

option. A written, recordable right to purchase a property under specified conditions, within a specified period of time.

option consideration. Payments made, usually in cash, to a property owner to maintain the right to purchase the property at the price stated in the *option*.

path of progress. Located in an area toward which development and industry are moving. For instance, a vacant lot that is said to be "in the path of progress" may be near the exit ramp of a soon-to-be-built highway, or adjacent to the site of an upcoming shopping center. Property that's in the path of progress can usually be expected to increase in value.

principal. 1. The amount of money raised by a *mortgage* or other loan, as opposed to the *interest* paid on it. **2.** The capital or main body of a financial holding.

promissory note. See *note*.

property tax. A government-imposed tax based on the *market value* of privately owned real estate. This is also called real estate tax.

Prudent Investor Rule. A legal doctrine that provides standards for choosing investments. As applied to the account holder of an IRA employer benefit plan, such as a *SEP-IRA* or a *SIMPLE plan,* it states that before making an investment, the account holder must consider similar alternative investments and choose the best one in terms of risk and return. This is sometimes called the Prudent Man Rule.

purchase agreement. See *contract of sale.*

raw land. Land that has no improvements such as utilities, landscaping, roads, drainage, and buildings. See also *improved land.*

real estate contract. See *land sale contract.*

Real Estate Investment Trust (REIT). A real estate mutual fund. The fund sells shares of ownership and uses the shareholders' money to buy, maintain, and sell real estate.

real estate tax. See *property tax.*

REIT. See *Real Estate Investment Trust.*

required minimum distribution (RMD). The minimum amount you must withdraw from your traditional IRA in a given year, once you reach the age of 70½. If your money is in a *Roth IRA,* no disbursement is required.

rollover. A tax-free transfer of money from one investment program to another.

Roth IRA. A type of *Individual Retirement Account* in which money is taxed as income the year it is contributed. Any gain, however, is not subject to income tax the year it is withdrawn.

Savings Incentive Match Plan for Employees (SIMPLE). A type of retirement plan that allows nongovernment employers in small businesses to set up retirement plans for their employees. Contributions are made by both the employee and the employer.

secured loan. A loan that is backed by *collateral,* such as real estate.

security instrument. A recorded document that allows real estate to be sold in the event of failure to fulfill an obligation or promise. A security instrument is more specifically called a *deed of trust* or *mortgage.*

self-directed IRA. An *Individual Retirement Account* whose administrator permits the account holder to choose the vehicles in which his funds are invested. These vehicles may include real estate, mutual funds, stocks and bonds, and other investments approved by the Internal Revenue Service. Any type of IRA—including *traditional IRAs, Roth IRAs,* and *Education IRAs*—can be self-directed.

SEP-IRA. See *Simplified Employee Pension.*

simple interest. Interest paid only on the *principal,* and not on any accumulated interest. See also *compound interest.*

SIMPLE plan. See *Savings Incentive Match Plan for Employees.*

Simplified Employee Pension (SEP). A type of retirement plan that allows nongovernment employers in small businesses to contribute to IRAs set up for their workers. The employees make no contribution.

soft equity. A contribution to the construction of property in the form of labor or services rather than cash. This is also called sweat equity. See also *hard equity.*

spec house. A single-family house built in anticipation of finding a buyer. The builder "speculates" that a buyer will be found.

speculative investing. Investing in *raw land* with the intent of actively pursuing its development, but with no identified end user for the finished product. Rather than investing in custom building for the buyer, the speculative investor anticipates that a demand already exists or will exist for the product, be it a house or a commercial building.

subdivision. A large parcel of land that's divided into individual lots.

sweat equity. See *soft equity.*

tax basis. The purchase price of a property, increased by improvements or decreased by depreciation.

tax lien. A legal claim placed on a property due to failure to pay property taxes.

tax roll. A list of all properties subject to taxation in a county or other jurisdiction. Among other facts, the list includes the assessed value of each property and the name of the property's owner.

tax sale. The sale of a property due to nonpayment of taxes.

tax sale certificate. A certificate sold by a county or other taxing unit when the owner of real estate is delinquent in paying his property taxes to the point that *foreclosure* is imminent. A tax sale certificate gives the buyer the right to collect lawful interest; to give proper notices to foreclose; to obtain possession of the property by court eviction; and to reside in, lease, rent, or dispose of the property at will.

tenancy-in-common ownership. A form of ownership in which each of two or more people has an undivided interest in a piece of property, without the right to survivorship. Because each person's interest, or share, is undivided, each can sell his share at any time without the consent or agreement of the other "tenants."

term. 1. The period of time during which something, such as a loan, is in effect. **2.** A condition specified in a legal agreement.

title. 1. The rights of ownership and possession of a particular property. **2.** The legal document that establishes the rights of ownership.

title insurance. A policy that protects the holder from any losses sustained by *defects in title*—in other words, against competing claims to a property's ownership.

title insurance company. A corporation that performs *title searches* and sells policies of insurance that guarantee the *title* to a property.

title report. A document that indicates the current status of a property's *title*. See also *title search*.

title search. The process of examining public records that relate to the ownership of a property to insure that the current owner has clear *title*, free of any *liens, mortgages,* or competing claims. The title search may be performed by an attorney, *title insurance company,* or other qualified title searcher, usually on behalf of the proposed purchaser of the property. In some states, found mostly on the East Coast and in the Midwest, the buyer's attorney prepares an *abstract of title,* which is a historical summary of the property's title that goes back to the first owner. In other states, typically found on the West Coast and in the Rocky Mountain region, the title company researches the property only to the last time the title report was issued.

traditional IRA. The most common type of *Individual Retirement Account,* in which money is tax-deductible the year it is contributed, but subject to income tax the year it is withdrawn.

triple-net lease. A lease in which the tenants pay all of the property's operating costs, including utilities, taxes, and insurance. The owner, then, receives a net rent.

trust. A legal entity created by the owner of property for the purpose of administering and distributing such property for the benefit of the owner and/or other persons, known as beneficiaries.

Uniform Lifetime Table. The table created by the IRS to calculate *required minimum distributions* when an IRA account holder is $70\frac{1}{2}$ or older, and is either unmarried or married to someone who is less than ten years younger.

Unrelated Business Income Tax (UBIT). A yearly tax levied on the income produced by IRA-purchased property that has related debt. Although originally created to affect charitable organizations, the UBIT is also applied to IRA investments. The first $1,000 of income is not subject to the tax. Any tax applied to the remaining income is determined by the relationship of the debt to the *tax basis* of the property.

yield. The return earned on an investment.

Resource List

Now that you have considered the many ways in which you can build IRA wealth through real estate investments, you may wish to start collecting your crew of professionals, or to learn more about the rules that regulate Individual Retirement Accounts. The groups and agencies listed below will help as you start your journey. (For a list of Selected IRA Trustees and Custodians, see page 227.)

BUSINESS BROKERS

International Business Brokers Association, Inc. (IBBA)
401 North Michigan Avenue, Suite 2200
Chicago, IL 60611-4267
Phone: 888-686-IBBA
Website: www.ibba.org/default.asp

This nonprofit organization offers an online service that will help you find a qualified business broker in your area.

FINANCIAL ADVISORS

Financial Planning Association
Phone: 800-322-4237
Website: www.fpanet.org

This association provides a list of certified financial planners in your area, as well as free information on financial planning.

National Association of Personal Financial Advisors (NAPFA)
3250 North Arlington Heights Road, Suite 109
Arlington Heights, IL 60004
Phone: 800-366-2732
Website: www.napfa.org/index.html

NAPFA offers referrals to fee-only (noncommission) financial planners in your area. All planners that belong to this association have at least two years' experience and at least one professional designation.

Society of Financial Service Professionals
270 S. Bryn Mawr Avenue
Bryn Mawr, PA 19010-2195
Phone: 610-526-2500
Website: www.financialpro.org

This society will send you the names of up to five members in your area.

IRA INFORMATION

Internal Revenue Service (IRS)
Phone: 800-TAX-FORM
Website: www.irs.gov/formspubs/index

IRS Publication 590, "Individual Retirement Arrangements (IRAs)"—which can be accessed online or ordered by mail—provides detailed information on IRAs, including guidelines for making withdrawals. The Joint Life and Last Survivor Expectancy table, needed to calculate required minimum distributions in some circumstances, appears at the end of the publication.

IRA Resource Associates, Inc.
418 NE Fourth Avenue, Suite 101
Camas, WA 98607-2128
Phone: 360-834-6689
Website: www.iraresource.com

IRA Resource Associates offers guidance for IRA owners interested in investing in real estate. The company's website presents a wealth of information about self-directed IRAs, Roth IRAs, and related topics.

Office of the Law Revision Counsel
Website: http://uscode.house.gov/usc.htm

This counsel prepares and publishes the United States Code, which is a consolidation and codification by subject matter of U.S. law. Visit the counsel's website to view or download titles and chapters of the U.S. Code, including Sections 408, 408A, and 4975 of Title 26, which present those codes that govern the establishment and use of Individual Retirement Accounts.

REAL ESTATE BROKERS

CCIM Institute
Website: www.ccim.com

The website of the CCIM Institute enables you to search for a CCIM (Certified Commercial Investment Member) by market area, property type, and specialization; or by city. Each member is a recognized professional in commercial real estate. CCIM also offers comprehensive courses in commercial real estate.

National Council of Exchangors (NCE)
Post Office Box 668
Morro Bay, CA 93443-0668
Phone: 800-324-1031
Website: www.nce1031.net/

This national nonprofit organization of real estate agents can, through its website, provide the names of Equity Marketing Specialists—agents who have achieved a high level of expertise in the field of real estate.

Selected IRA Trustees and Custodians

Throughout *IRA Wealth,* you have learned the importance of working with an experienced IRA administrator that can assist you in making real estate investments through a self-directed retirement plan. Although for simplicity I have used the term "administrator" throughout this book, as you learned in Chapter 3, you actually need a trustee or custodian with administrative capabilities. The following partial list will guide you to a number of excellent companies that can help build IRA wealth.

American Church Trust Company
14615 Benfer Road
Houston, TX 77069
Phone: 800-228-8825
Website: www.churchtrust.com

CNA Trust Corporation
3080 South Bristol Street, 2nd FL
Costa Mesa, CA 92626
Phone: 800-274-8798
Website: www.cnatrust.com

First Trust Corporation
Phone: 800-525-2124
Website: www.firsttrust.com

Lincoln Trust
PO Box 5831
Denver, CO 80217
Phone: 800-825-2501
Website: www.lincolntrust.com

PENSCO Trust Company
250 Montgomery Street, 3rd FL
San Francisco, CA 94104
Phone: 800-969-4472
Website: www.pensco.com

Sterling Trust Company
PO Box 2526
Waco, TX 76702
Phone: 800-955-3434
Website: www.sterling-trust.com

Internal Revenue Service Codes on IRAs

Throughout *IRA Wealth*, I have discussed the basics of those government codes that govern IRA investments. If you wish to study these rules in full, or if you wish to provide your crew with this material, you will find the text of United States Codes Title 26, Sections 408A and 4975—the two most important codes to understand when making IRA investments—presented below. Refer to Section 408A for general rules on Roth IRAs, and Section 4975 for rules on prohibited transactions. If you wish to view further government codes—including Section 408, which presents general IRA rules—search the website of the Office of the Law Revision Counsel at http://uscode.house.gov/usc.htm. For basic information on IRA regulations presented in layman's terms, visit the IRS website. (See the Resource List on page 224.)

Title 26—Internal Revenue Code
Section 408A. Roth IRAs

TITLE 26 - INTERNAL REVENUE CODE
Subtitle A - Income Taxes
CHAPTER 1 - NORMAL TAXES AND SURTAXES
Subchapter D - Deferred Compensation, Etc.
PART I - PENSION, PROFIT-SHARING, STOCK BONUS PLANS, ETC.
Subpart A - General Rule
-HEAD-
Sec. 408A. Roth IRAs

-STATUTE-

(a) General rule

Except as provided in this section, a Roth IRA shall be treated for purposes of this title in the same manner as an individual retirement plan.

(b) Roth IRA

For purposes of this title, the term "Roth IRA" means an individual retirement plan (as defined in section 7701(a)(37)) which is designated (in such manner as the Secretary may prescribe) at the time of establishment of the plan as a Roth IRA. Such designation shall be made in such manner as the Secretary may prescribe.

(c) Treatment of contributions

(1) No deduction allowed

No deduction shall be allowed under section 219 for a contribution to a Roth IRA.

(2) Contribution limit

The aggregate amount of contributions for any taxable year to all Roth IRAs maintained for the benefit of an individual shall not exceed the excess (if any) of -

(A) the maximum amount allowable as a deduction under section 219 with respect to such individual for such taxable year (computed without regard to subsection (d)(1) or (g) of such section), over

(B) the aggregate amount of contributions for such taxable year to all other individual retirement plans (other than Roth IRAs) maintained for the benefit of the individual.

(3) Limits based on modified adjusted gross income

(A) Dollar limit

The amount determined under paragraph (2) for any taxable year shall not exceed an amount equal to the amount determined under paragraph (2)(A) for such taxable year, reduced (but not below zero) by the amount which bears the same ratio to such amount as -

(i) the excess of -

(I) the taxpayer's adjusted gross income for such taxable year, over

(II) the applicable dollar amount, bears to

(ii) $15,000 ($10,000 in the case of a joint return or a married individual filing a separate return).

The rules of subparagraphs (B) and (C) of section 219(g)(2)

shall apply to any reduction under this subparagraph.

(B) Rollover from IRA

A taxpayer shall not be allowed to make a qualified rollover contribution to a Roth IRA from an individual retirement plan other than a Roth IRA during any taxable year if, for the taxable year of the distribution to which such contribution relates -

(i) the taxpayer's adjusted gross income exceeds $100,000, or

(ii) the taxpayer is a married individual filing a separate return.

(C) Definitions

For purposes of this paragraph -

(i) adjusted gross income shall be determined in the same manner as under section 219(g)(3), except that -

(I) any amount included in gross income under subsection (d)(3) shall not be taken into account; and

(II) any amount included in gross income by reason of a required distribution under a provision described in paragraph (5) shall not be taken into account for purposes of subparagraph (B)(i), and

(ii) the applicable dollar amount is -

(I) in the case of a taxpayer filing a joint return, $150,000,

(II) in the case of any other taxpayer (other than a married individual filing a separate return), $95,000, and

(III) in the case of a married individual filing a separate return, zero.

(D) Marital status

Section 219(g)(4) shall apply for purposes of this paragraph.

(4) Contributions permitted after age 70½

Contributions to a Roth IRA may be made even after the individual for whom the account is maintained has attained age 70½.

(5) Mandatory distribution rules not to apply before death

Notwithstanding subsections (a)(6) and (b)(3) of section 408 (relating to required distributions), the following provisions shall not apply to any Roth IRA:

(A) Section 401(a)(9)(A).

(B) The incidental death benefit requirements of section 401(a).

(6) Rollover contributions

(A) In general

No rollover contribution may be made to a Roth IRA unless it is a qualified rollover contribution.

(B) Coordination with limit

A qualified rollover contribution shall not be taken into account for purposes of paragraph (2).

(7) Time when contributions made

For purposes of this section, the rule of section 219(f)(3) shall apply.

(d) Distribution rules

For purposes of this title -

(1) Exclusion

Any qualified distribution from a Roth IRA shall not be includible in gross income.

(2) Qualified distribution

For purposes of this subsection -

(A) In general

The term "qualified distribution" means any payment or distribution -

(i) made on or after the date on which the individual attains age 59$\frac{1}{2}$,

(ii) made to a beneficiary (or to the estate of the individual) on or after the death of the individual,

(iii) attributable to the individual's being disabled (within the meaning of section 72(m)(7)), or

(iv) which is a qualified special purpose distribution.

(B) Distributions within nonexclusion period

A payment or distribution from a Roth IRA shall not be treated as a qualified distribution under subparagraph (A) if such payment or distribution is made within the 5-taxable year period beginning with the first taxable year for which the individual made a contribution to a Roth IRA (or such individual's spouse made a contribution to a Roth IRA) established for such individual.

(C) Distributions of excess contributions and earnings

The term "qualified distribution" shall not include any distribution of any contribution described in section 408(d)(4) and any net income allocable to the contribution.

(3) Rollovers from an IRA other than a Roth IRA

(A) In general

Notwithstanding section 408(d)(3), in the case of any

distribution to which this paragraph applies -

(i) there shall be included in gross income any amount which would be includible were it not part of a qualified rollover contribution,

(ii) section 72(t) shall not apply, and

(iii) unless the taxpayer elects not to have this clause apply for any taxable year, any amount required to be included in gross income for such taxable year by reason of this paragraph for any distribution before January 1, 1999, shall be so included ratably over the 4-taxable year period beginning with such taxable year.

Any election under clause (iii) for any distributions during a taxable year may not be changed after the due date for such taxable year.

(B) Distributions to which paragraph applies

This paragraph shall apply to a distribution from an individual retirement plan (other than a Roth IRA) maintained for the benefit of an individual which is contributed to a Roth IRA maintained for the benefit of such individual in a qualified rollover contribution.

(C) Conversions

The conversion of an individual retirement plan (other than a Roth IRA) to a Roth IRA shall be treated for purposes of this paragraph as a distribution to which this paragraph applies.

(D) Additional reporting requirements

Trustees of Roth IRAs, trustees of individual retirement plans, or both, whichever is appropriate, shall include such additional information in reports required under section 408(i) as the Secretary may require to ensure that amounts required to be included in gross income under subparagraph (A) are so included.

(E) Special rules for contributions to which 4-year averaging applies

In the case of a qualified rollover contribution to a Roth IRA of a distribution to which subparagraph (A)(iii) applied, the following rules shall apply:

(i) Acceleration of inclusion

(I) In general

The amount required to be included in gross income for each of the first 3 taxable years in the 4-year period under subparagraph (A)(iii) shall be increased by the

aggregate distributions from Roth IRAs for such taxable
year which are allocable under paragraph (4) to the portion
of such qualified rollover contribution required to be
included in gross income under subparagraph (A)(i).
(II) Limitation on aggregate amount included
   The amount required to be included in gross income for
any taxable year under subparagraph (A)(iii) shall not
exceed the aggregate amount required to be included in
gross income under subparagraph (A)(iii) for all taxable
years in the 4-year period (without regard to subclause
(I)) reduced by amounts included for all preceding taxable
years.
 (ii) Death of distributee
   (I) In general
   If the individual required to include amounts in gross
income under such subparagraph dies before all of such
amounts are included, all remaining amounts shall be
included in gross income for the taxable year which
includes the date of death.
   (II) Special rule for surviving spouse
   If the spouse of the individual described in subclause
(I) acquires the individual's entire interest in any Roth
IRA to which such qualified rollover contribution is
properly allocable, the spouse may elect to treat the
remaining amounts described in subclause (I) as includible
in the spouse's gross income in the taxable years of the
spouse ending with or within the taxable years of such
individual in which such amounts would otherwise have been
includible. Any such election may not be made or changed
after the due date for the spouse's taxable year which
includes the date of death.
 (F) Special rule for applying section 72
  (i) In general
   If -
     (I) any portion of a distribution from a Roth IRA is
properly allocable to a qualified rollover contribution
described in this paragraph; and
     (II) such distribution is made within the 5-taxable year
period beginning with the taxable year in which such
contribution was made,
  then section 72(t) shall be applied as if such portion were

includible in gross income.

(ii) Limitation

Clause (i) shall apply only to the extent of the amount of the qualified rollover contribution includible in gross income under subparagraph (A)(i).

(4) Aggregation and ordering rules

(A) Aggregation rules

Section 408(d)(2) shall be applied separately with respect to Roth IRAs and other individual retirement plans.

(B) Ordering rules

For purposes of applying this section and section 72 to any distribution from a Roth IRA, such distribution shall be treated as made -

(i) from contributions to the extent that the amount of such distribution, when added to all previous distributions from the Roth IRA, does not exceed the aggregate contributions to the Roth IRA; and

(ii) from such contributions in the following order:

(I) Contributions other than qualified rollover contributions to which paragraph (3) applies.

(II) Qualified rollover contributions to which paragraph (3) applies on a first-in, first-out basis.

Any distribution allocated to a qualified rollover contribution under clause (ii)(II) shall be allocated first to the portion of such contribution required to be included in gross income.

(5) Qualified special purpose distribution

For purposes of this section, the term "qualified special purpose distribution" means any distribution to which subparagraph (F) of section 72(t)(2) applies.

(6) Taxpayer may make adjustments before due date

(A) In general

Except as provided by the Secretary, if, on or before the due date for any taxable year, a taxpayer transfers in a trustee-to-trustee transfer any contribution to an individual retirement plan made during such taxable year from such plan to any other individual retirement plan, then, for purposes of this chapter, such contribution shall be treated as having been made to the transferee plan (and not the transferor plan).

(B) Special rules

(i) Transfer of earnings

Subparagraph (A) shall not apply to the transfer of any

contribution unless such transfer is accompanied by any net income allocable to such contribution.

(ii) No deduction

Subparagraph (A) shall apply to the transfer of any contribution only to the extent no deduction was allowed with respect to the contribution to the transferor plan.

(7) Due date

For purposes of this subsection, the due date for any taxable year is the date prescribed by law (including extensions of time) for filing the taxpayer's return for such taxable year.

(e) Qualified rollover contribution

For purposes of this section, the term "qualified rollover contribution" means a rollover contribution to a Roth IRA from another such account, or from an individual retirement plan, but only if such rollover contribution meets the requirements of section 408(d)(3). For purposes of section 408(d)(3)(B), there shall be disregarded any qualified rollover contribution from an individual retirement plan (other than a Roth IRA) to a Roth IRA.

(f) Individual retirement plan

For purposes of this section -

(1) a simplified employee pension or a simple retirement account may not be designated as a Roth IRA; and

(2) contributions to any such pension or account shall not be taken into account for purposes of subsection (c)(2)(B).

-SOURCE-

(Added Pub. L. 105-34, title III, Sec. 302(a), Aug. 5, 1997, 111 Stat. 825; amended Pub. L. 105-206, title VI, Sec. 6005(b)(1)-(7), (9), title VII, Sec. 7004(a), July 22, 1998, 112 Stat. 796-800, 833; Pub. L. 105-277, div. J, title IV, Sec. 4002(j), Oct. 21, 1998, 112 Stat. 2681-908.)

Title 26—Internal Revenue Code
Section 4975. Tax on Prohibited Transactions

TITLE 26 - INTERNAL REVENUE CODE
Subtitle D - Miscellaneous Excise Taxes
CHAPTER 43 - QUALIFIED PENSION, ETC., PLANS

-HEAD-

Sec. 4975. Tax on prohibited transactions

-STATUTE-

(a) Initial taxes on disqualified person

There is hereby imposed a tax on each prohibited transaction. The rate of tax shall be equal to 15 percent of the amount involved with respect to the prohibited transaction for each year (or part thereof) in the taxable period. The tax imposed by this subsection shall be paid by any disqualified person who participates in the prohibited transaction (other than a fiduciary acting only as such).

(b) Additional taxes on disqualified person

In any case in which an initial tax is imposed by subsection (a) on a prohibited transaction and the transaction is not corrected within the taxable period, there is hereby imposed a tax equal to 100 percent of the amount involved. The tax imposed by this subsection shall be paid by any disqualified person who participated in the prohibited transaction (other than a fiduciary acting only as such).

(c) Prohibited transaction

(1) General rule

For purposes of this section, the term "prohibited transaction" means any direct or indirect -

(A) sale or exchange, or leasing, of any property between a plan and a disqualified person;

(B) lending of money or other extension of credit between a plan and a disqualified person;

(C) furnishing of goods, services, or facilities between a plan and a disqualified person;

(D) transfer to, or use by or for the benefit of, a disqualified person of the income or assets of a plan;

(E) act by a disqualified person who is a fiduciary whereby he deals with the income or assets of a plan in his own interests or for his own account; or

(F) receipt of any consideration for his own personal account by any disqualified person who is a fiduciary from any party dealing with the plan in connection with a transaction involving the income or assets of the plan.

(2) Special exemption

The Secretary shall establish an exemption procedure for purposes of this subsection. Pursuant to such procedure, he may grant a conditional or unconditional exemption of any disqualified person or transaction, orders of disqualified persons or transactions, from all or part of the restrictions imposed by paragraph (1) of this subsection. Action under this subparagraph may be taken only after consultation and coordination with the Secretary of Labor. The Secretary may not grant an exemption under this paragraph unless he finds that such exemption is -

(A) administratively feasible,

(B) in the interests of the plan and of its participants and beneficiaries, and

(C) protective of the rights of participants and beneficiaries of the plan.

Before granting an exemption under this paragraph, the Secretary shall require adequate notice to be given to interested persons and shall publish notice in the Federal Register of the pendency of such exemption and shall afford interested persons an opportunity to present views. No exemption may be granted under this paragraph with respect to a transaction described in subparagraph (E) or (F) of paragraph (1) unless the Secretary affords an opportunity for a hearing and makes a determination on the record with respect to the findings required under subparagraphs (A), (B), and (C) of this paragraph, except that in lieu of such hearing the Secretary may accept any record made by the Secretary of Labor with respect to an application for exemption under section 408(a) of title I of the Employee Retirement Income Security Act of 1974.

(3) Special rule for individual retirement accounts

An individual for whose benefit an individual retirement account is established and his beneficiaries shall be exempt from the tax imposed by this section with respect to any transaction concerning such account (which would otherwise be taxable under this section) if, with respect to such transaction, the account ceases to be an individual retirement account by reason of the application of section 408(e)(2)(A) or if section 408(e)(4) applies to such account.

(4) Special rule for Archer MSAs

An individual for whose benefit an Archer MSA (within the meaning of section 220(d)) is established shall be exempt from the tax imposed by this section with respect to any transaction concerning such account (which would otherwise be taxable under this section) if section 220(e)(2) applies to such transaction.

(5) Special rule for education individual retirement accounts

An individual for whose benefit an education individual retirement account is established and any contributor to such account shall be exempt from the tax imposed by this section with respect to any transaction concerning such account (which would otherwise be taxable under this section) if section 530(d) applies with respect to such transaction.

(d) Exemptions

Except as provided in subsection (f)(6), the prohibitions provided in subsection (c) shall not apply to -

(1) any loan made by the plan to a disqualified person who is a participant or beneficiary of the plan if such loan -

(A) is available to all such participants or beneficiaries on a reasonably equivalent basis,

(B) is not made available to highly compensated employees (within the meaning of section 414(q)) in an amount greater than the amount made available to other employees,

(C) is made in accordance with specific provisions regarding such loans set forth in the plan,

(D) bears a reasonable rate of interest, and

(E) is adequately secured;

(2) any contract, or reasonable arrangement, made with a disqualified person for office space, or legal, accounting, or other services necessary for the establishment or operation of the plan, if no more than reasonable compensation is paid therefor;

(3) any loan to an (FOOTNOTE 1) leveraged employee stock ownership plan (as defined in subsection (e)(7)), if -

(FOOTNOTE 1) So in original. Probably should be "a".

(A) such loan is primarily for the benefit of participants and beneficiaries of the plan, and

(B) such loan is at a reasonable rate of interest, and any collateral which is given to a disqualified person by the plan consists only of qualifying employer securities (as defined in subsection (e)(8));

(4) the investment of all or part of a plan's assets in deposits which bear a reasonable interest rate in a bank or similar financial institution supervised by the United States or a State, if such bank or other institution is a fiduciary of such plan and if -

(A) the plan covers only employees of such bank or other institution and employees of affiliates of such bank or other institution, or

(B) such investment is expressly authorized by a provision of the plan or by a fiduciary (other than such bank or institution or affiliates thereof) who is expressly empowered by the plan to so instruct the trustee with respect to such investment;

(5) any contract for life insurance, health insurance, or annuities with one or more insurers which are qualified to do business in a State if the plan pays no more than adequate consideration, and if each such insurer or insurers is -

(A) the employer maintaining the plan, or

(B) a disqualified person which is wholly owned (directly or indirectly) by the employer establishing the plan, or by any person which is a disqualified person with respect to the plan, but only if the total premiums and annuity considerations written by such insurers for life insurance, health insurance, or annuities for all plans (and their employers) with respect to which such insurers are disqualified persons (not including premiums or annuity considerations written by the employer maintaining the plan) do not exceed 5 percent of the total premiums and annuity considerations written for all lines of insurance in that year by such insurers (not including premiums or annuity considerations written by the employer maintaining the plan);

(6) the provision of any ancillary service by a bank or similar financial institution supervised by the United States or a State, if such service is provided at not more than reasonable compensation, if such bank or other institution is a fiduciary of such plan, and if -

(A) such bank or similar financial institution has adopted adequate internal safeguards which assure that the provision of such ancillary service is consistent with sound banking and financial practice, as determined by Federal or State supervisory authority, and

(B) the extent to which such ancillary service is provided is subject to specific guidelines issued by such bank or similar financial institution (as determined by the Secretary after consultation with Federal and State supervisory authority), and under such guidelines the bank or similar financial institution does not provide such ancillary service -

(i) in an excessive or unreasonable manner, and

(ii) in a manner that would be inconsistent with the best interests of participants and beneficiaries of employee benefit plans;

(7) the exercise of a privilege to convert securities, to the extent provided in regulations of the Secretary but only if the plan receives no less than adequate consideration pursuant to such conversion;

(8) any transaction between a plan and a common or collective trust fund or pooled investment fund maintained by a disqualified person which is a bank or trust company supervised by a State or Federal agency or between a plan and a pooled investment fund of an insurance company qualified to do business in a State if -

(A) the transaction is a sale or purchase of an interest in the fund,

(B) the bank, trust company, or insurance company receives not more than a reasonable compensation, and

(C) such transaction is expressly permitted by the instrument under which the plan is maintained, or by a fiduciary (other than the bank, trust company, or insurance company, or an affiliate thereof) who has authority to manage and control the assets of the plan;

(9) receipt by a disqualified person of any benefit to which he may be entitled as a participant or beneficiary in the plan, so long as the benefit is computed and paid on a basis which is consistent with the terms of the plan as applied to all other participants and beneficiaries;

(10) receipt by a disqualified person of any reasonable compensation for services rendered, or for the reimbursement of expenses properly and actually incurred, in the performance of his duties with the plan, but no person so serving who already receives full-time pay from an employer or an association of employers, whose employees are participants in the plan or from an employee organization whose members are participants in such plan shall receive compensation from such fund, except for reimbursement of expenses properly and actually incurred;

(11) service by a disqualified person as a fiduciary in addition to being an officer, employee, agent, or other representative of a disqualified person;

(12) the making by a fiduciary of a distribution of the assets of the trust in accordance with the terms of the plan if such

assets are distributed in the same manner as provided under section 4044 of title IV of the Employee Retirement Income Security Act of 1974 (relating to allocation of assets);

(13) any transaction which is exempt from section 406 of such Act by reason of section 408(e) of such Act (or which would be so exempt if such section 406 applied to such transaction) or which is exempt from section 406 of such Act by reason of section 408(b)(12) of such Act;

(14) any transaction required or permitted under part 1 of subtitle E of title IV or section 4223 of the Employee Retirement Income Security Act of 1974, but this paragraph shall not apply with respect to the application of subsection (c)(1) (E) or (F); or

(15) a merger of multiemployer plans, or the transfer of assets or liabilities between multiemployer plans, determined by the Pension Benefit Guaranty Corporation to meet the requirements of section 4231 of such Act, but this paragraph shall not apply with respect to the application of subsection (c)(1) (E) or (F).

(e) Definitions

(1) Plan

For purposes of this section, the term "plan" means -

(A) a trust described in section 401(a) which forms a part of a plan, or a plan described in section 403(a), which trust or plan is exempt from tax under section 501(a),

(B) an individual retirement account described in section 408(a),

(C) an individual retirement annuity described in section 408(b),

(D) an Archer MSA described in section 220(d),

(E) an education individual retirement account described in section 530, or

(F) a trust, plan, account, or annuity which, at any time, has been determined by the Secretary to be described in any preceding subparagraph of this paragraph.

(2) Disqualified person

For purposes of this section, the term "disqualified person" means a person who is -

(A) a fiduciary;

(B) a person providing services to the plan;

(C) an employer any of whose employees are covered by the plan;

(D) an employee organization any of whose members are covered by the plan;

(E) an owner, direct or indirect, of 50 percent or more of -

(i) the combined voting power of all classes of stock entitled to vote or the total value of shares of all classes of stock of a corporation,

(ii) the capital interest or the profits interest of a partnership, or

(iii) the beneficial interest of a trust or unincorporated enterprise,

which is an employer or an employee organization described in subparagraph (C) or (D);

(F) a member of the family (as defined in paragraph (6)) of any individual described in subparagraph (A), (B), (C), or (E);

(G) a corporation, partnership, or trust or estate of which (or in which) 50 percent or more of -

(i) the combined voting power of all classes of stock entitled to vote or the total value of shares of all classes of stock of such corporation,

(ii) the capital interest or profits interest of such partnership, or

(iii) the beneficial interest of such trust or estate,

is owned directly or indirectly, or held by persons described in subparagraph (A), (B), (C), (D), or (E);

(H) an officer, director (or an individual having powers or responsibilities similar to those of officers or directors), a 10 percent or more shareholder, or a highly compensated employee (earning 10 percent or more of the yearly wages of an employer) of a person described in subparagraph (C), (D), (E), or (G); or

(I) a 10 percent or more (in capital or profits) partner or joint venturer of a person described in subparagraph (C), (D), (E), or (G).

The Secretary, after consultation and coordination with the Secretary of Labor or his delegate, may by regulation prescribe a percentage lower than 50 percent for subparagraphs (E) and (G) and lower than 10 percent for subparagraphs (H) and (I).

(3) Fiduciary

For purposes of this section, the term "fiduciary" means any person who -

(A) exercises any discretionary authority or discretionary

control respecting management of such plan or exercises any authority or control respecting management or disposition of its assets,

(B) renders investment advice for a fee or other compensation, direct or indirect, with respect to any moneys or other property of such plan, or has any authority or responsibility to do so, or

(C) has any discretionary authority or discretionary responsibility in the administration of such plan.

Such term includes any person designated under section 405(c)(1)(B) of the Employee Retirement Income Security Act of 1974.

(4) Stockholdings

For purposes of paragraphs (2)(E)(i) and (G)(i) there shall be taken into account indirect stockholdings which would be taken into account under section 267(c), except that, for purposes of this paragraph, section 267(c)(4) shall be treated as providing that the members of the family of an individual are the members within the meaning of paragraph (6).

(5) Partnerships; trusts

For purposes of paragraphs (2)(E)(ii) and (iii), (G)(ii) and (iii), and (I) the ownership of profits or beneficial interests shall be determined in accordance with the rules for constructive ownership of stock provided in section 267(c) (other than paragraph (3) thereof), except that section 267(c)(4) shall be treated as providing that the members of the family of an individual are the members within the meaning of paragraph (6).

(6) Member of family

For purposes of paragraph (2)(F), the family of any individual shall include his spouse, ancestor, lineal descendant, and any spouse of a lineal descendant.

(7) Employee stock ownership plan

The term "employee stock ownership plan" means a defined contribution plan -

(A) which is a stock bonus plan which is qualified, or a stock bonus and a money purchase plan both of which are qualified under section 401(a), and which are designed to invest primarily in qualifying employer securities; and

(B) which is otherwise defined in regulations prescribed by the Secretary.

A plan shall not be treated as an employee stock ownership plan unless it meets the requirements of section 409(h), section 409(o), and, if applicable, section 409(n) and section 664(g) and, if the employer has a registration-type class of securities (as defined in section 409(e)(4)), it meets the requirements of section 409(e).

(8) Qualifying employer security

The term "qualifying employer security" means any employer security within the meaning of section 409(l). If any moneys or other property of a plan are invested in shares of an investment company registered under the Investment Company Act of 1940, the investment shall not cause that investment company or that investment company's investment adviser or principal underwriter to be treated as a fiduciary or a disqualified person for purposes of this section, except when an investment company or its investment adviser or principal underwriter acts in connection with a plan covering employees of the investment company, its investment adviser, or its principal underwriter.

(9) Section made applicable to withdrawal liability payment funds

For purposes of this section -

(A) In general

The term "plan" includes a trust described in section 501(c)(22).

(B) Disqualified person

In the case of any trust to which this section applies by reason of subparagraph (A), the term "disqualified person" includes any person who is a disqualified person with respect to any plan to which such trust is permitted to make payments under section 4223 of the Employee Retirement Income Security Act of 1974.

(f) Other definitions and special rules

For purposes of this section -

(1) Joint and several liability

If more than one person is liable under subsection (a) or (b) with respect to any one prohibited transaction, all such persons shall be jointly and severally liable under such subsection with respect to such transaction.

(2) Taxable period

The term "taxable period" means, with respect to any prohibited transaction, the period beginning with the date on which the prohibited transaction occurs and ending on the earliest of -

(A) the date of mailing a notice of deficiency with respect to the tax imposed by subsection (a) under section 6212,

(B) the date on which the tax imposed by subsection (a) is assessed, or

(C) the date on which correction of the prohibited transaction is completed.

(3) Sale or exchange; encumbered property

A transfer or real or personal property by a disqualified person to a plan shall be treated as a sale or exchange if the property is subject to a mortgage or similar lien which the plan assumes or if it is subject to a mortgage or similar lien which a disqualified person placed on the property within the 10-year period ending on the date of the transfer.

(4) Amount involved

The term "amount involved" means, with respect to a prohibited transaction, the greater of the amount of money and the fair market value of the other property given or the amount of money and the fair market value of the other property received; except that, in the case of services described in paragraphs (2) and (10) of subsection (d) the amount involved shall be only the excess compensation. For purposes of the preceding sentence, the fair market value -

(A) in the case of the tax imposed by subsection (a), shall be determined as of the date on which the prohibited transaction occurs; and

(B) in the case of the tax imposed by subsection (b), shall be the highest fair market value during the taxable period.

(5) Correction

The terms "correction" and "correct" mean, with respect to a prohibited transaction, undoing the transaction to the extent possible, but in any case placing the plan in a financial position not worse than that in which it would be if the disqualified person were acting under the highest fiduciary standards.

(6) Exemptions not to apply to certain transactions

(A) In general

In the case of a trust described in section 401(a) which is part of a plan providing contributions or benefits for employees some or all of whom are owner-employees (as defined in section 401(c)(3)), the exemptions provided by subsection (d) (other than paragraphs (9) and (12)) shall not apply to a transaction in which the plan directly or indirectly -

(i) lends any part of the corpus or income of the plan to,

(ii) pays any compensation for personal services rendered to the plan to, or

(iii) acquires for the plan any property from, or sells any property to,

any such owner-employee, a member of the family (as defined in section 267(c)(4)) of any such owner-employee, or any corporation in which any such owner-employee owns, directly or indirectly, 50 percent or more of the total combined voting power of all classes of stock entitled to vote or 50 percent or more of the total value of shares of all classes of stock of the corporation.

(B) Special rules for shareholder-employees, etc.

(i) In general

For purposes of subparagraph (A), the following shall be treated as owner-employees:

(I) A shareholder-employee.

(II) A participant or beneficiary of an individual retirement plan (as defined in section 7701(a)(37)).

(III) An employer or association of employees which establishes such an individual retirement plan under section 408(c).

(ii) Exception for certain transactions involving shareholder-employees

Subparagraph (A)(iii) shall not apply to a transaction which consists of a sale of employer securities to an employee stock ownership plan (as defined in subsection (e)(7)) by a shareholder-employee, a member of the family (as defined in section 267(c)(4)) of such shareholder-employee, or a corporation in which such a shareholder-employee owns stock representing a 50 percent or greater interest described in subparagraph (A).

(C) Shareholder-employee

For purposes of subparagraph (B), the term "shareholder-employee" means an employee or officer of an S corporation who owns (or is considered as owning within the meaning of section 318(a)(1)) more than 5 percent of the outstanding stock of the corporation on any day during the taxable year of such corporation.

(g) Application of section

This section shall not apply -

(1) in the case of a plan to which a guaranteed benefit policy (as defined in section 401(b)(2)(B) of the Employee Retirement Income Security Act of 1974) is issued, to any assets of the insurance company, insurance service, or insurance organization merely because of its issuance of such policy;

(2) to a governmental plan (within the meaning of section 414(d)); or

(3) to a church plan (within the meaning of section 414(e)) with respect to which the election provided by section 410(d) has not been made.

In the case of a plan which invests in any security issued by an investment company registered under the Investment Company Act of 1940, the assets of such plan shall be deemed to include such security but shall not, by reason of such investment, be deemed to include any assets of such company.

(h) Notification of Secretary of Labor

Before sending a notice of deficiency with respect to the tax imposed by subsection (a) or (b), the Secretary shall notify the Secretary of Labor and provide him a reasonable opportunity to obtain a correction of the prohibited transaction or to comment on the imposition of such tax.

(i) Cross reference

For provisions concerning coordination procedures between Secretary of Labor and Secretary of the Treasury with respect to application of tax imposed by this section and for authority to waive imposition of the tax imposed by subsection (b), see section 3003 of the Employee Retirement Income Security Act of 1974.

Index

RETIRING RIGHT, THIRD EDITION
Planning for a Successful Retirement
Lawrence J. Kaplan

Everybody dreams of a "golden retirement"—carefree times, financial security, and good health. But without the proper planning, that dream can turn into a nightmare. *Retiring Right* was developed to provide you with all the facts you need to design your own individual retirement plan so that you can make your special dream a reality.

Written by Dr. Lawrence J. Kaplan, one of the country's leading experts in retirement planning, this practical book answers all your most important questions about savings and investment income, the Social Security system, and so much more. Each section covers a particular area of concern, including lifestyle issues such as working, leisure, and housing; long-term retirement funding, including savings and investments and pensions; day-to-day financial considerations, such as budgeting and taxes; life and health insurance; and preparing for the inevitable through estate planning, wills, and trusts. All information reflects the latest regulations so that you can take full advantage of the newest tax laws and maximize your retirement income.

Through planning guides and worksheets, *Retiring Right* helps you apply successful retirement strategies to meet your individual needs. These guides allow you to evaluate your financial situation, select and implement the means by which you can achieve financial security, and chart your course towards a fulfilling and secure retirement.

$17.95 US/$28.95 CAN • 396 pages • 7.5 x 9-inch quality paperback • 2-Color
Personal Finance/Retirement • ISBN 0-7570-0132-7

HOW TO FINANCE ANY REAL ESTATE, ANY PLACE, ANY TIME

Strategies That Work

James A. Misko

Ever wonder how real estate magnates become real estate magnates? By filling out mind-numbing mortgage applications? By making personal guarantees to their bankers? Hardly. For many years, successful real estate investors have used nontraditional methods of securing funding. They have created effective money strategies that circumvent banks, yet result in highly profitable deals. Now, real estate professional James Misko makes these innovative techniques available to the general public in his upcoming book *How to Finance Any Real Estate, Any Place, Any Time.*

In this easy-to-use guide, Jim offers fifty-three time-tested nontraditional ways of buying properties. These are not pie-in-the-sky theories about what could happen "if," but proven deal-closing secrets that will put the wraps on virtually any real estate purchase. In this book, you will learn how to turn your dwindling stocks into real estate equities, how to exchange property for property tax-free, how to acquire land without money, and so much more.

How to Finance Any Real Estate, Any Place, Any Time provides you with all the information you might pay hundreds of dollars for through realty courses, at only a fraction of the cost. If the only thing holding you back from buying your dream house or investment property is financing, maybe it's time to buy "outside the box."

Available December 2003 • $17.95 U.S./$28.95 CAN • 168 pages
6 x 9-inch quality paperback • SBN 0-7570-0135-1